From the Ghost in the Box

to

Successful

Biofeedback Training

Robert Shellenberger, Ph.D.

and

Judith Alyce Green, Ph.D.

Health Psychology Publications

FROM THE GHOST IN THE BOX TO SUCCESSFUL BIOFEEDBACK TRAINING

ROBERT SHELLENBERGER, *Ph.D.*
and
JUDITH ALYCE GREEN, *Ph.D.*

RC
489
.B53
S54
1986

HEALTH PSYCHOLOGY PUBLICATIONS

Copyright • 1986
by Robert Shellenberger, Ph.D., and Judith Green, Ph.D.
All rights reserved.

No part of this book may be reproduced without written permission from the publisher, except by a reviewer who may quote brief passages or reproduce illustrations in a review; nor may any part of this book be reproduced, stored in a retrieval system, or transmitted in any form or by any means electronic, mechanical, photocopying, recording, or other, without written permission from the authors.

This book is manufactured in the United States of America.
It has been typeset and printed by Pioneer Press.
Published by Health Psychology Publications,
710 11th Avenue, Suite 106
Greeley, Colorado.

First Printing—March, 1986
Second Printing—July, 1987
Third Printing—August, 1988

Library of Congress Catalog Card Number: 86-82415
ISBN 0-9617145-0-6

Table of Contents

Preface v
Acknowledgements vii

1

Models of Biofeedback Training 1
Conceptualizations of Biofeedback 1
Biofeedback Research Models 4
The Official Doctrine 6
Category Mistake 7
Category Mistakes and the Ghost in the Box 7
Consequences of the Official Doctrine and Category
    Mistakes 10

2

Methodological and Conceptual Errors 13
Error #1: Insufficient number of training sessions 13
        Table 1: Studies with minimal training 14
Error #2: Insufficient length of each training session ... 16
Error #3: Homework exercises are not given 17
Error #4: Failure to maximize internal locus
        of control 19
Error #5: Failure to provide adequate
        cognitive support 22
Error #6: Double-blind designs.................... 25
Error #7: Failure to establish training criteria 30
Error #8: Using a relaxation control group for
        comparison to biofeedback training 35
Error #9: Failure to incorporate mental/emotional
        variables in biofeedback training 39

Error #10: Failure to establish reliability measures
and confidence bands 43
Figure 1: EMG Confidence Bands 45
Error #11: Failure to control for adaptation 48
The Mastery Model 50
Error #12: Failure to train to mastery 50

3
Unsuccessful Biofeedback Training 55

4
Successful Biofeedback Training 57
Essential Hypertension and Biofeedback Training......58
Table 2, Successful Clinical Biofeedback
Training for Essential Hypertension......59
Biofeedback Training for Treatment of Headache......64
Table 3, Successful Clinical Biofeedback
Training for Migraine, Tension,
& Mixed Headache 64
Tension Headache 67
Migraine Headache 68
Raynaud's Disease and Biofeedback Training 69
Biofeedback Training for other Disorders 69
Applied Clinical Biofeedback Studies and the Mastery
Model 70
The Mastery Model 70
Clinical Biofeedback Practice 73
Table 4, Systematic Case Studies 76
Table 5, Follow-Up Studies 81

5
The Tomato Effect, The Placebo Effect, and Science 85
The Tomato Effect 85
Confounding Variables 87
Specific vs. Non-specific Effects 91
The Placebo Effect 92
Control Groups 93
There is No Sugar Effect 96
Science 98

6
From the Ghost in the Box to Successful Biofeedback Training 103
Self Regulation Training 108
Conclusion 110

About the Authors 113
References 115

Preface

The history of this document flows from symposium presentation, to lengthy article, to monograph. This final form has evolved over months of trying to make it shorter.

It began in 1984 in preparation for the Biofeedback Society of America Annual Meeting. The theme of the meeting was "Biofeedback in Perspective—Fifteen Years of Development." In keeping with that theme, Bob created a symposium titled, "When Does Biofeedback Training Succeed and When Does it Fail?"

In reviewing the literature, Bob found that many biofeedback studies have failed and for a variety of reasons. In most cases, minimal training was given and subjects failed to learn. A pattern became apparent: studies that provided minimal training assume an innate power in the biofeedback instrument, and from that came the title of Bob's presentation on the panel, "From the Ghost in the Box to Successful Biofeedback Training."

To clarify the puzzle of poor biofeedback research, Bob reread *The Concept of Mind* by Gilbert Ryle. The concept of the category mistake is developed in detail in that book. A category mistake occurs when concepts appropriate to one category are inappropriately applied to another category. The category mistake helped to clarify the impression that faulty conceptualizations are at the core of problems in biofeedback research. This was strikingly verified in articles by Hatch (1982 and 1983) in which biofeedback is described as having specific, innate effects like a drug. With this clue to a drug model approach to biofeedback training, we searched the literature again and found that a drug model is indeed prevalent and is a common model "when biofeedback fails."

In reviewing the literature we were also immediately confronted with a model of biofeedback training more extensively used than the drug model, the operant conditioning model derived from animal learning. These models appeared to be different, but in analyzing them carefully, we found that both assume "specific effects" of biofeedback that can and should be studied independently of trainee variables such as expectations, instructions, and relaxation. We found that certain research methods, and designs derived from these models, often prevent the demonstration of the efficacy of biofeedback training because they prevent learning.

At the same time, the other half of the symposium presentation, " . . . to Successful Biofeedback Training" generated considerable thought about the elements of training that lead to successful learning and symptom reduction. Our own research and clinical practice in biofeedback training were of value because we had already developed successful training protocols.

The need to carefully and critically analyze the conceptualizations, models, research designs, data and conclusions underlying both unsuccessful and successful biofeedback training became certain as we discussed these issues for the 1984 conference. After the conference we could not put the topic down. Our candid disapproval of much of biofeedback training research, and the confusion in the field of biofeedback training, spurred us on. Over the months we studied biofeedback training literature and spent hours discussing the issues. Gradually, written material emerged.

At a fortuitous time, when we were bogged down under the weight of ideas and discouraged of ever having a critique of this type published, an article appeared in *The American Psychologist* (August, 1985) that rekindled our determination to clarify the issues, "for once and for all" and to hastily complete this document. The author wrote: "With respect to training, I can only conclude that clinical training no longer prepares psychologists to think critically, or, if it does, that this intellectual skill is not being used by practitioners in the area of biofeedback" (Roberts, 1985, p. 938). And "There is absolutely no convincing evidence that biofeedback is an essential or specific technique for the treatment of any condition'' (p. 940).

This monograph is an answer to claims of this sort, and explains why researchers like Roberts have both confused, and been confused by the field of biofeedback training. We believe that this monograph makes a unique contribution to the field by defining the major problem as *conceptual* and secondarily as empirical. Other authors have stated that the main problem in biofeedback is the lack of good research (Yates, 1980; Gatchel and Price, 1979; White and Tursky, 1982). We argue that the problems are primarily related to conceptual errors concerning the nature of biofeedback training and the nature of scientific research.

In the detailed analysis of conceptualizations about biofeedback training, and the ramifications of these conceptualizations in research, we provide a framework for understanding many conflicting results and conclusions regarding the efficacy of biofeedback training. This framework includes twelve methodological errors that occur repeatedly in biofeedback research, and distinguishes between trial-and-error learning in biofeedback, referred to as *unsystematic* biofeedback training, and *systematic* biofeedback training that includes the use of systematic training techniques. Finally, we develop a model of biofeedback training that eliminates these errors and ensures masterful self regulation through thorough training—the mastery model.

In the development of the mastery model, we examine successful biofeedback training studies, and describe the reasons for researchers' continued disregard of successful work, a phenomenon called "the tomato effect." The familiar concepts of "confounding variable," "nonspecific effects," "placebo effect," and "unscientific" are critiqued. We challenge the belief that the only form of rigorous scientific research in biofeedback is to isolate an independent variable, external to the trainee, and control for confounding variables. We argue that it is precisely this belief that resulted in the pursuit of a nonexistent entity—the specific effect of biofeedback—the ghost in the box.

We hope that this monograph will provide a guide to researchers, clinicians, and reviewers of the field of biofeedback training. And we dedicate this work to all who are involved in the evolution of self regulation therapy.

Acknowledgements

We gratefully acknowledge the review of sections of this document by Elmer E. Green, Ph.D., The Menninger Foundation, Topeka, Kansas. To our friend and colleague, Pat McCary, Ph.D., we give special thanks for encouragement and editorial assistance. We thank Aims Community College, Greeley, Colorado for its excellent research facilities and John Turner for his personal support. We appreciate the editorial assistance of Gene Frederick, Dave Werner, Frank Gordon, Ph.D., and T. Robnett. And we thank each other for our patience and persistence.

1

Models of Biofeedback Training

The model or set of models a psychologist believes in determines to a great extent, the kind of research he does, and the type of explanations he develops.
Introduction to Experimental Psychology,
Matheson, Bruce, and Beauchamp, 1974

Science advances by conceptualization and experimentation. Inappropriate concepts and models result in poor experimental design, unsuccessful research, and years of wasted time and effort. Appropriate conceptualizations and models can result in the rapid development of an emerging science.

Our first task is to determine an appropriate model for biofeedback training. Our second task is to examine current conceptualizations and designs that underlie biofeedback research. *Our thesis is that, with a few notable exceptions, biofeedback research has lacked clear and appropriate conceptualizations and has lacked appropriate experimental design.*

Conceptualizations of Biofeedback

An Appropriate Model

What is an appropriate model for biofeedback training? Is biofeedback like a drug? Is it like training a rat? Is it like training an athlete to excel in a sport or teaching a student skills, or is biofeedback something else altogether? The answer depends on how biofeedback training and the goals of biofeedback training are conceptualized.

In the early days of biofeedback, excitement and interest were sparked by a clear goal: biofeedback training would be a tool with which individuals could gain voluntary self regulation of various psychophysiological processes. The interest in self regulation was expressed in titles chosen for the publications, *Biofeedback and Self-Control* (Aldine Books) and *Biofeedback and Self-Regulation*, the Journal of the Biofeedback Society of America. Self regulation was fascinating, since the autonomic nervous system and aspects of the somatic are considered "involuntary." In addition, self regulation was potentially of great benefit for symptom reduction in the treatment of psychosomatic disease. It was exciting to find that by using information feedback, trainees could learn to regulate psychophysiological processes without drugs.

What is the nature of this tool called biofeedback training? Biofeedback training is the use of instruments to feed back psychophysiological information to a person. The information is referred to as "psychophysiological" because psychological processes are reflected in physiological functioning. Biofeedback instruments are designed to monitor, amplify and feed back a variety of biological processes such as heart rate, blood pressure, muscle tension, blood flow in the hands and feet, and brain waves. The trainee uses the information from her/his body to learn to make changes in the psychophysiological process being monitored. The information is helpful in learning to regulate mind and body in the same way that information from the dart board is helpful in learning to play darts. The trainee uses the information to become conscious of, and voluntarily create, the physiological and psychological states that produce the desired physiological change. The key here is consciousness because consciousness is necessary for psychophysiological self regulation. And the key to consciousnesss is feedback of information.

Two analogies have been used to describe the function of biofeedback *instrumentation*. One analogy describes the instrumentation as *removing a blindfold*. "This use of instrumentation is analogous to removing the blindfold from the novice who is trying to shoot a basket . . . If our novice basketball player were blindfolded, so that he did not have the feedback of seeing whether he was succeeding or failing, he could not learn" (Miller, 1975, p. 367). Without information feedback, learning cannot occur. This is true in sports, education, social learning, and certainly in biofeedback training in which the trainee is attempting to gain voluntary control of a normally involuntary, "blindfolded," and unconscious process.

A *mirror* is the other appropriate and often used analogy to describe the function of the biofeedback instrument. Like a mirror, the instrument enhances consciousness and psychophysiological self regulation by reflecting the psychophysiological process being regulated. Like a mirror the only requirement of the instrument is that it provides a true reflection, i.e. useable and accurate information. Like a mirror, the usefulness of the biofeedback instrument is dependent upon how the information from it is used. Like a mirror, the biofeedback instrument has no inherent power to create change. The human using the biofeedback mirror has the power to control the process being reflected.

When the mirror characteristics of the biofeedback instrument are understood, the rest of the model unfolds: the trainee uses the information to gain self regulation of these processes, and learning progresses either through trial-and-error, or learning progresses through systematic training.

Biofeedback *training* is the *process* of mastering psychophysiological self regulation skills, with the aid of information from a biofeedback instrument, and is similar to skills learning in any activity such as sports, music or education. This is the model that we develop in this manuscript; we refer to it as the "mastery model."

The *essential ingredients of biofeedback training* are those of training in any complex skill: clear goals, rewards for approximating the goals, enough time and practice for learning, proper instructions, a variety of training techniques, and feedback of information. The *essential "ingredients" of the user* of the information from the biofeedback machine are those of any learner of a complex skill: consciousness, cognitive understanding, language, positive expectations, motivation, and positive interaction with the coach, teacher, or therapist. The implications of this model for biofeedback training, in clinical practice, and in research are vast.

To a large extent, biofeedback as a mirror, and biofeedback training as mastery of self regulation skills, are concepts that have been accepted by biofeedback clinicians. With a few notable exceptions, occurring early in the history of biofeedback research and recently, these concepts and their implications have not been accepted by researchers.

Biofeedback Research Models

In our review of over 300 theoretical papers and research reports on biofeedback training, we find that the most common conceptualizations of biofeedback training are derived from two models: (1) operant conditioning with laboratory animals and (2) specific effects of drugs.

The Operant Conditioning Model.

Many of the early biofeedback studies were done by researchers trained in operant conditioning methodology with laboratory animals, such as Benson, Kimmel, Miller, Shapiro, Sterman, Taub, and Tursky. These researchers applied the *methods, language, and goals of animal research to biofeedback training with humans.* The procedures are described as: "sensorimotor EEG operant conditioning" (Sterman, 1977); "operant electrodermal modification" (Shapiro & Watanabe, 1972); "learned control of human cardiovascular integration through operant conditioning" (Schwartz, Shapiro, & Tursky, 1971); "classical and operant conditioning in the enhancement of biofeedback" (Furedy & Riley, 1982); "operant conditioning of heart rate slowing" (Engel & Hansen, 1971).

Using the operant conditioning model of learning, researchers focus on concepts such as the *stimulus:* "the goal is to bring [biofeedback subjects] under some degree of stimulus control" (Alexander, 1975, p. 216); the *reinforcer:* "among the strategies suggested [for the study of the active treatment effect of biofeedback] were delaying reinforcement, varying reinforcement schedules . . . " (Katkin & Goldband, 1979, p. 186); "You can see that feedback did help subjects maintain a higher skin temperature than subjects who did not have feedback . . . It looks like biofeedback acts like a reinforcer here and that subjects who do not have it seem to be extinguishing more rapidly than subjects who do" (Surwit, 1982, p. 240); and the *contingency* between stimulus and response: "With biofeedback, however, I think we have been somehow uniquely blessed. No matter whether one conceives of the process of biofeedback training as operant conditioning, motor skills learning, or self control in a purely phenomenological sense, it is the contingency between biological behavior and the feedback stimulus that all theories predict is responsible for determining change" (Hatch, 1982, p. 381). And biofeedback is effective "if and only if it is shown that it is the contingency between the target behavior (HRD) [heart rate deceleration] and the reinforcement (i.e., information or feedback about HRD) that is responsible for the increase in HRD" (Furedy, 1979, p. 83).

Furthermore, some researchers assume direct parallels between human learning and laboratory animal learning. To explain the methods and poor results of their study with Raynaud's patients, Guglielmi, Roberts and Patterson (1982) write:

> A third argument that could be used to challenge the results of this study might be that the subjects' ignorance of the feedback-relevant response inherent in double-blind studies necessarily led to inadequate training and therefore to negative findings. The success in training animals, obviously unaware of the target response, to control a variety of autonomic functions would seem to invalidate this contention (Guglielmi et al., 1982, p. 117).

The argument is that since laboratory animals are "unconscious of the target response" then obviously humans need not be aware either. The conditions that apply to rats also apply to humans.

The Drug Model

"The removal of the contingency between biofeedback and behavior is logically similar to removing the active ingredient from a medicine" (Hatch, Klatt, Fitzgerald, Jashewy, & Fisher, 1983,

p. 411). "In this regard, pharmacological medicine provides an appropriate model for treatment evaluation." (Furedy, 1985, p. 159). Application of the drug model to biofeedback training results in conceptual issues and research designs unique to the model that have occurred repeatedly in biofeedback research. It is assumed that like a drug, biofeedback has "specific effects" and that these specific effects must be demonstrated independently of any "nonspecific" effects. In addition, the drug model insists that the placebo effect is a hazard to the study of the specific effects of biofeedback, and must be controlled for or eliminated (Beatty, 1982; Furedy, 1985; Katkin & Goldband, 1979; Miller, 1976; Price, 1979).

To study these specific drug-like effects, designs appropriate to drug research are adopted for the study of biofeedback, primarily the double-blind design, (Hatch et al., 1983; Guglielmi, Roberts & Patterson, 1982). "The function of the double-blind arrangement is that it separates placebo effects from specific effects" (Furedy, 1985, p. 159).

The Official Doctrine

A combination of concepts taken from drug effects and animal research models has prevailed in biofeedback research, so much so that we call it the "official doctrine." The "official doctrine" approach has been the scientific model in biofeedback research, and is still rewarded by research funding, publications, and university degrees. But are the concepts of the official doctrine derived from drug and animal models applicable to biofeedback training? The answer to this question is crucial.

To assess the applicability of the official doctrine to biofeedback training the models must be examined conceptually and empirically. *Empirically,* we must examine the research methodology, results and conclusions that follow from the models of the official doctrine. *Conceptually,* we must examine whether or not the conceptualizations, the language, and the goals of the models accurately describe the phenomena being studied. The latter task is facilitated by employing a concept that has evolved from the history of science, the *category mistake.*

Category Mistake

The concept of "category mistake" is useful in analyzing the conceptualizations that underlie biofeedback training (Hesse, 1970; Ryle, 1949; Ryle, 1965). A category mistake occurs when conceptualizations appropriate to one category are inaccurately applied to another. Anton Mesmer made a category mistake in his explanation of hypnosis. This is illustrated in the investigation of his powers by a group of distinguished scientists attempting to determine the veracity of Mesmer's claim that he had access to a powerful healing force. The scientists set up an experiment in which a sick boy was brought to Mesmer to heal. Mesmer said that the healing power could be put into a tree and when the boy touched the tree he would be healed. The boy was told that he would be healed, and he was healed, but he touched the wrong tree. The scientists concluded that Mesmer was a fake. Mesmer's category mistake was to apply a concept from the category of matter, magnetism, to the properties of an interactive process between human beings. The scientists also made a category mistake by concluding that Mesmer was a fake, thus dismissing an important phenomenon. As a result of these category mistakes, hypnotherapy was prevented from reaching its full fruititon for many years (Frankel, 1976).

In the initial investigation of new phenomena, category mistakes are likely because familiar conceptualizations appropriate to known phenomena are inaccurately applied. The category mistakes are often subtle and difficult to recognize because they appear to be correct. As attempts have been made to develop and understand biofeedback training through research, category mistakes have been made that arise from faulty conceptualizations.

Category Mistakes and the Ghost in the Box

The essence of the official doctrine derived from drug and animal models is that the biofeedback instrument, or "biofeedback" when this means merely the use of a machine, has an *inherent power with specific effects*. These effects are either like a drug, as in the drug model, or like the stimulus, reinforcer or contingency, as in the operant conditioning model. "In summary, stimuli have innate and acquired properties which enable them to control behavior" (Engel, 1979, p. 171). To conceptualize biofeedback in this way is to make a category mistake. The biofeedback instrument is merely a mirror that provides information. It has no inherent power to create change or control behavior. It would be a category mistake, indeed superstitious, to believe that a mirror has power, and it is a category mistake and superstititous to believe that biofeedback has a special "specific" power to create change. This belief is superstitious because it assumes causality where none exists. It was superstitious to believe that Halley's Comet caused the death of the king because the king died when the comet was overhead, and it is superstitious to believe that the biofeedback instrument, or its signal characteristics, cause behavior change when the human creating the change is using a biofeedback instrument.

A characteristic of information is that it has no power independently of the *user,* the *user's goals,* and the *environment of the user.* An uninterested general psychology student who is required to participate in a biofeedback experiment may find the biofeedback information boring. A tension headache patient, however, may find EMG information rewarding because *her goal* is to reduce her pain. But it would be a category mistake to believe that the "biofeedback mirror" has an inherent and specific effect that brings behavior under its control.

A second category mistake arises from applying a simplistic model of operant conditioning to biofeedback training. We noted in the discussion of the operant conditioning model that researchers have attributed behavior change through biofeedback training to a variety of variables—the stimulus, the reinforcer, the contingency between stimulus and response, or the contingency between the response and the reinforcer. To suggest that behavior change through biofeedback training is determined or controlled by these variables, is to borrow concepts appropriate to one category, operant conditioning with laboratory animals, and apply it to another category, human learning. This is a category mistake. The category "rodent" is different from the category "human" and the category "animal learning" is *ipso facto* different from the category "human learning." Consequently laboratory research with animals is categorically different from research with humans. Unlike rats, humans are not microcephalic, they have self awareness, and they bring to research complex and uncontrolled variables: (1) environment, e.g. job and family stressors, insurance reimbursements, and workman's compensation; (2) an elaborate language; (3) beliefs and expectations; (4) motivation; (5) and a host of psychophysiological and somatic illnesses for which they are seeking treatment. This enumeration of human characteristics as evidence of the categorical difference between humans and rodents may seem obvious. Nevertheless, in "official doctrine" research these differences are not taken into account or are purposefully ignored.

Working with rats and pigeons, experimenters have derived principles of learning that appear to govern behavior. Indeed in animal laboratory settings operant conditioning theory may apply, and perhaps its application to humans is appropriate in understanding and treating particular cases, such as the mentally retarded, infants, phobic, and impulsive patients. And it is certain that reinforcement motivates behavior acquisition. However, while learning to peck at a green dot and not a red one, or learning to run a complicated maze, or jump through a hoop, may represent the absolute pinnacle of animal learning, *responses conditioned to external stimuli represent the most rudimentary form of human learning.* When operant conditioning theory is applied to human learning in biofeedback training, the most rudimentary form of learning is studied through the methodology of the model. The theories, goals and methods appropriate to the pinnacle of human learning—higher mathematics, virtuoso musical performance, gold medal ice skating, and self regulation of a complex psychophysiological process—are ignored. Bar-pressing behavior becomes the model for human learning: "It will be noted that, just as biofeedback can be formulated in terms of operant conditioning or in terms of voluntary control, so the lever-pressing example could have been formulated as either operant lever-press conditioning with light as reinforcement or as the rats' voluntarily "emitting" lever presses "in order to get" the light" (Furdey & Riley, 1982, p. 84).

Because these models conceptualize "biofeedback" as having a specific drug-like effect, or innate or acquired properties like stimuli and reinforcers, and assume an inherent power that does not exist, we call them the *"ghost in the box"* approaches to biofeedback training.

In summary, our thesis is that the official doctrine incorporates two major category mistakes:

Category Mistake #1: equating the properties of objects such as drugs with information processing by humans of signals from the biofeedback instrument;

Category Mistake #2: equating animal learning with human learning, the latter involving goals, cognitive and emotional processes, language, and complex uncontrolled environmental variables.

Consequences of the Official Doctrine and Category Mistakes

To determine the appropriateness of the official doctrine models *empirically,* we must examine the research methodology that is derived from the models. We propose that at least twelve conceptual and methodological errors arise from the category mistakes of the official doctrine. These errors are not mutually exclusive. They are interrelated and produce similar research results and conclusions, because they are derived from common category mistakes. The interrelationship of these errors and the need to analyze them carefully and precisely leads to recurrent themes in our discussion. We believe that this is useful in helping to clarify the issues and problems in biofeedback research. These errors contribute to unsuccessful biofeedback training and have hindered the development of the field and its acceptance in the scientific and medical communities.

In Chapter Two, we examine the twelve conceptual and methodological errors and the research results and faulty generalizations derived from them.

We then briefly examine the conceptualizations and methods that underlie successful biofeedback training. A training model appropriate to the goal of maximizing psychophysiological self regulation and symptom reduction is proposed in Chapter Two, and developed in detail in Chapter Four. We refer to this as the "mastery model." The model incorporates concepts and methods of high performance training of athletes. As in athletic training, mastery is the *sine qua non* for successful biofeedback training.

2

Methodological and Conceptual Errors

> The official doctrine has been injudiciously applied to biofeedback training with humans. The consequence of the category mistakes is poorly designed research because the conception of biofeedback training is like Mesmer's "Ghost in the Tree" mythology in which biofeedback is viewed as having an independent power that is quite magical, namely, the Ghost in the Box.

Methodology Error #1: **Insufficient number of training sessions.**
Conceptual Error: **The feedback "stimulus" has such magical power that its effectiveness can be measured after subjects have been briefly exposed to this power (Category Mistake #1).**

In the double-blind study by Hatch et al. (1983), one training session was given. The authors conclude, "the second prediction that subjects given true biofeedback would show lower EMG levels compared to subjects given pseudofeedback was not supported. There were no significant differences in EMG levels among the four groups at any stage of training" (p. 422). This type of study, using one to four sessions, is representative of many studies that have confused the field of biofeedback training by implying that biofeedback is so powerful that minimal training is needed. Of 167 voluntary heart rate studies, *75% gave only one to three sessions* (Banderia, Bouchard, & Granger, 1982, p. 323). Examples of minimal training are presented in Table 1, excluding heart rate studies.

Table 1
Studies with Minimal Training

Number of Sessions	Modality	Author
One	EMG	Segreto-Bures & Kotses, 1984
Three	BP	Erbeck, Elfner & Driggs, 1983
One	EMG	Hatch, et al., 1983
Four	EMG	Morasky, Reynolds, & Sowell, 1983
Two	Temp	Suter, Fredericson, & Portuesi, 1983
Two	EMG	Shirley, Burish, & Rowe, 1982
One	EMG	Kiffer, Fridlun, & Fowler, 1981
One	BP	Lutz & Holmes, 1981
Three	EMG	O'Connell & Yeaton, 1981
One	EMG	Uchiyama, Lutterjohann & Shah, 1981
Three	EMG	Davis, 1980
Two	BV	Hoon, 1980
Four	EMG	Nielsen & Holmes, 1980
Three	GSR	Volow, Erwin, & Cipolat, 1979
Three	BP	Shannon, Goldman, & Lee, 1978
Two	EEG	Plotkin, 1977
Three	EMG	Stern & Berrenberg, 1977
Three	Temp	Willerman, Skeen, & Simpson, 1977
Four	BP	Blanchard, Haynes, Kallman, & Harkey, 1976
One	EEG	Plotkin, & Cohen, 1976
One	EEG	Plotkin, Mazer, & Loewy, 1976
One	Temp	Price & Tursky, 1976
Two	FPV	Simpson & Nelson, 1976
Three	EMG	Alexander, 1975
Two	EMG/EEG	DeGood & Chisholm, 1978
Three	BP	Fey & Lindholm, 1976
One	EMG	Haynes, Mosley, & McGowan, 1975
One	EEG	Lynch, Paskewitz, & Orne, 1974
One	EEG	Beatty, 1972
One	GSC	Klinge, 1972
One	GSR	Shapiro & Watanabe, 1972
One	BP	Shapiro, Tursky, Gershon, & Stern, 1971
One	SPL	Crider, Shapiro, & Tursky, 1971
One	SPL	Johnson, & Schwartz, 1971
One	EMG	Cleaves, 1970

Note. Abbreviations: electromyogram (EMG); electroencephalogram (EEG); blood pressure (BP); temperature (Temp); blood volume (BV); galvanic skin resistance (GSR); galvanic skin conductance (GSC); skin potential level (SPL); finger pulse volume (FPV).

Based on minimal training, the logical fallacy of "hasty generalization" is frequent. Manuck, Levenson, Hinrichsen, and Gryll (1975) state: "The present findings, while demonstrating significant bi-directional heart-rate changes, do not support the hypothesis that feedback facilitates voluntary heart-rate control . . . Thus it may be speculated that the case for feed-back assisted heart rate control has been somewhat overstated in the recent literature" (p. 300). On the basis of one training session the authors speculate on the inefficacy of heart-rate feedback.

Plotkin's research (1977 and 1976) has been widely cited for demonstrating that alpha feedback does not contribute to relaxation or tranquility. "Thus it appears that the major contribution that alpha feedback makes to the attainment of meditative-like experiences is the supply of a setting which is conducive to the natural self-inducement of such states" (Plotkin & Cohen, 1976, p. 21). Plotkin arrives at this conclusion on the basis of one EEG session in two studies (Plotkin et. al., 1976 and Plotkin & Cohen, 1976) and two EEG sessions in a third study (Plotkin, 1977).

Another experimenter writes, "The lack of a more convincing group learning effect across sessions was puzzling in view of the moderately extended practice" (Volow, et al. 1979, p. 139). Three sessions of skin resistance feedback were given. On a basis of four 20 minute forehead EMG treatment sessions, compared to relaxation and no-treatment control groups, Nielsen and Holmes (1980) conclude: ". . . it appears that the use of EMG biofeedback to teach normal persons how to control arousal in threatening situations may not be clearly warranted" (p. 247).

Following a sports model, this paucity of training is like attempting to train an athlete to run a four minute mile in four sessions and then conclude that human beings are unable to run the four minute mile and that furthermore, *the stopwatch is not useful.*

Methodology Error #2: **Insufficient length of each training session.**
Conceptual Error: The magical biofeedback box has such power that length of "exposure" to the box during a session can be of very short duration (Category Mistake #1).

Many biofeedback training sessions reported in the research literature are only 16, 10, or even 3 minutes in length. Representative studies using a minimum of 3 to 16 minutes are: Borgeat, Hade, Larouche, and Bedwani (1980); Davis, (1980); Dahlström, Carlsson, Gale, and Jansson (1984); Herzfield and Taub (1980); Kostes, Rapaport, and Glaus (1978); Lang, P. J. (1977); McCanne, (1983); Nielson and Holmes, (1980); Uchiyama, Lutterjohann, and Shah (1981); Williamson, Janell, Margueolot, and Hutchinson (1983); Wilson and Bird (1981). Often total minutes of training are divided into "trials," a method borrowed from animal research. For example Davis (1980) provided ten 70-second trials with twenty second intervals of EMG training. Nielson and Holmes (1980) provided sixteen one-minute trials with 15 second intervals. Other researchers have required subjects to alternately increase or decrease the variable on successive trials, such as heart rate (Twentyman and Lang, 1980), or hand temperature (Suter, Fredericson, and Portuesi, 1983). Commenting on EEG methodology, Hardt (1975) argued that such training is like trying to get an airplane off the ground by taxiing first forward and then backward repeatedly.

In a widely cited article, Lang (1977) concludes, " . . . I think the available data justify the conclusion that high density visceral feedback does not provide a uniquely powerful treatment for anxiety or other broad system stress responses" (p. 329). Lang bases this conclusion on heart rate data from his laboratory and on EMG and heart rate data from studies done in his laboratory by Cuthbert (1976). Lang fails to note that in Cuthbert's study subjects were given *five fifteen minute EMG sessions and trained with eyes open while looking at an oscilloscope*. Besides failing to critique Cuthbert's methodology, Lang generalizes from the subjects of Cuthbert's study to a patient population that would be given EMG training under very different conditions and would not be trained to lower forehead EMG with eyes open looking at an oscilloscope.

Methodology Error #3: **Homework exercises are not given.** *Conceptual Error:* **Homework is not needed since the power is in the machine which is used only in the laboratory or clinic (Category Mistakes #1 and #2).**

Biofeedback researchers have rarely required trainees to do home biofeedback training. In over 300 research studies on EMG, thermal, heart rate, blood pressure and GSR feedback training only about 15% reported *recommending* homework practice. To date, few studies have reported home *training* data. In some cases the suggestion for homework is no more than "practice at home what you are doing in the laboratory."

The failure to incorporate homework exercises into biofeedback research results from attributing power to the instrument. The drug model assumes a "specific effect" of the treatment being studied. Any variable that affects the outcome independently of the specific effect "confounds" the results and must be eliminated. Therefore, when the drug model is applied to biofeedback research, homework cannot be given because homework is a "confounding" variable and data on the "specific effect" of biofeedback are invalidated. "Blanchard and Young were forced to conclude that while the data looked promising, the unique contribution of EMG feedback had been consistently confounded with both the inclusion of other relaxation methods during training and regular home practice of nonfeedback relaxation" (Alexander & Smith, 1979, p. 125).

The failure to give homework in biofeedback research arises also from Category Mistake #2. In conditioning studies the animal does not practice the desired response when returned to the cage. Failure to give "home practice" arises from the animals inability to comprehend language and also from the operant conditioning paradigm in which the stimulus and reinforcement are thought to control behavior (Methodological Error #4). The animal is not expected to demonstrate the behavior in the home cage, where stimulus and reinforcers are absent.

In applying concepts from operant conditioning to biofeedback training, in which the stimulus and reinforcer ghosts in the box are thought to have power, home practice for humans is excluded. According to theory, training can proceed only while the trainee is connected to the box, and biofeedback instruments are typically not given to subjects for home use. The experiments of Budzynski, Stoyva, Adler, and Jullaney (1973), Sargent, Walters, and Green (1973), Sterman and MacDonald (1978) are early exceptions to this practice.

Failure to provide the subject or patient with home practice exercises with or without an instrument has hindered the development of biofeedback training; we comment on this again in Error #8 (use of relaxation control groups). Skilled athletes cannot achieve competence without regular practice, nor can biofeedback trainees. In most cases, training in the laboratory or the clinic is not sufficient for learning self regulation skills and for transfer of training to other situations. Homework is an integral part of successful training.

hand warming came under the control of the hypothalamus, the limbic system, the cortex, or the trainee. The error here seems obvious—green lights do not have the power to increase hand temperature any more than red traffic lights have the power to make us apply the brakes. The human who is increasing hand temperature, or braking at a red light has the power to control the response.

In biofeedback training neither the feedback instrument nor the information nor the contingency between the information and the response have the power to control the response, just as they do not have the power to control the response when we use a mirror. In biofeedback training the locus of control is internal, just as it is when we use a mirror. The trainee alone has the power to use the information, learn the desired response, and control that response. Furthermore, the human controls the contingency in the same way that the human controls the contingency between stimulus and response when using a mirror. The human controls the contingency because the human controls the response, which in turn produces the "feedback stimulus." For example, if you put your right hand over your left ear while looking in a mirror, you will see exactly that movement reflected in the mirror. The reflection of that response acts as a stimulus for new behavior, as a reinforcer, and as information simultaneously, *and all are under your control because you initiate the behavior.* It would be superstitious to believe that the mirror caused you to put your hand over your ear. Similarily, in learning digital blood flow control with biofeedback for example, we create an internal state, and we see the immediate response on the meter. The reflection is simultaneously the stimulus, the response, the information, and the reinforcer. At the same time, we also become aware of the contingency between the internal state that we voluntarily create and the physiological response that is indicated by the feedback.

This *commonality of the stimulus, reinforcer, information and response is unique to biofeedback training* and sets it apart from operant conditioning; they are not in the same category of learning paradigms. If this discussion seems abstruse simply stand in front of a mirror, perform any task, and ask yourself "What is controlling what?"

The assumption that behavior change through biofeedback train-

Methodology Error #4: **Failure to maximize internal locus of control.**
Conceptual Error: **The response is under the control of the feedback characteristics: stimulus, reinforcer, and contingency (Category Mistakes #1 and #2).**

In their book on behavioral medicine under the heading "Operant Conditioning," Olton and Noonberg (1980) state, "Biofeedback teaches a person to develop voluntary control over some biological process. In this respect, it is a form of learning, differing from other forms mainly in the types of responses that are controlled" (p. 24). These authors are suggesting that human learning is like research animal learning—humans use the same strategies and are subject to the same situational and psychological variables as laboratory animals; the main difference in biofeedback training is that the human is not learning bar-pressing or disc-pecking. In accordance with this category mistake, and in spite of using the term "voluntary," the authors continue, "*To be effective in controlling behavior* [emphasis added], reinforcers must be made contingent upon behavior" (p. 24). As noted in Chapter 1, other authors suggest that the behavior comes under the control of the stimulus, (Alexander, 1975; Engel, 1979). We also noted that Hatch (1982) and Furedy and Riley (1982) believe that the contingency between the stimulus and response determines behavior.

The language of "control" and "determines" is a statement of causality. In operant conditioning the stimulus, reinforcer and contingency are external experimental variables, not subject variables and as noted, are thought to control or cause behavior. Thus the locus of control is thought to be external to the subject. It is important to note that in animal research the locus of control *is* external to the animal in so far as the *researcher* has the power to control stimuli, reinforcers, and the contingencies between stimuli, responses and reinforcers. For this reason an external locus of control is assumed and promoted in biofeedback research with humans.

Applying the language of these models literally it would be said, "Hand warming came under the control of the green light" when a green light signals hand warming. It would not be stated that

ing is controlled by a power external to the trainee leads to serious methodological problems in research. *When the feedback characteristics (stimulus, reinforcer, information, and contingency) are believed to control the response, or the feedback is believed to have a specific drug-like effect, the human in the situation is disempowered, learning is thwarted due to lack of clear goals, proper instruction, home practice and coaching, and the most rudimentary form of learning is studied.*

In applying the myth of external locus of control to running, it would be assumed for example, that the stopwatch has the power to control the runner's behavior. If the coach believed this, training of the athlete would be minimal; the coach would focus on the characteristics of the stopwatch, rather than on physical, emotional and mental training techniques. This has happened repeatedly in biofeedback training research. Numerous research articles have been written on "stimulus characteristics," "response characteristics," "contingency characteristics," and "reinforcement characteristics" (Katkin & Goldband, 1979, p. 186). A natural consequence of this mythology is a paucity of studies on the uniquely human parameters involved in successful learning. Furthermore, research based on the ghost in the box mythology fails, not because biofeedback training fails, or because humans cannot learn to self regulate, but because there is no magic in the box. The "magic" is in the human using the box.

Methodology Error #5: **Failure to provide adequate cognitive support (rationales, instructions and coaching).**
Conceptual Error: **The biofeedback machine has such power that minimal instruction and coaching are needed; trial-and-error learning is good enough, (Category Mistake #1). Instruction is not needed in drug and animal studies, and therefore is not needed in biofeedback training with humans (Category Mistake #2).**

In their article, "An Alternative Perspective on Biofeedback Efficacy Studies: A Reply to Steiner and Dince," Kewman and Roberts (1983) defend the use of unskilled trainers in biofeedback training studies. They take this stance because they do not believe that high performance coaching is necessary for the "power" of biofeedback training to have its effect. The concept of the biofeedback "technician" implies that the power is in the box and only a technician is needed for connecting the subject or patient to the instrument and turning it on, and it implies that trial-and-error learning is good enough for the effect of biofeedback to be demonstrated.

When researchers attempt to study the biofeedback ghost in the box devoid of facilitating variables such as instructions, coaching, and appropriate rationales, we call this "bare bones biofeedback," the same term adopted by Budzynski (1973a) to describe this research approach. As an example of bare bones biofeedback, consider the familiar research scenario: the thermister is taped to the subject's finger with the instruction, "Your task is to make the needle move to the right; I will return in ten minutes at the end of the experiment." Twentyman and Lang (1980) describe their procedure: "Subjects were encouraged to work seriously at the task but were not advised how to accomplish it" (p. 421). Stoffer, Jensen and Nesset (1979) write, "Each subject was told that when the red "start" light came on he was to attempt to raise his finger temperature by whatever mental means he could employ for a 13 minute period" (p. 555). In these situations the only learning strategy available to the subject is trial-and-error, not a high-powered strategy.

In human performance training such as sports or music, students are not expected to learn a skill solely by trial-and-error. Or imagine letting a teenager learn to drive a car by trial-and-error, "Here are the keys, just turn on the engine and see what happens." At least it is clear that the car has no special power to instill driving skills in the learner, just as the biofeedback machine has no special power. Many biofeedback studies, however, give the impression that to provide instructions or coach the subject, or enhance performance in any way would bias the results—as though the power of the entity, biofeedback, could and should be studied independently of any skills of the user of the biofeedback information. Using bare bones methodology, the minimal potential of feedback to facilitate psychophysiological change and learning is studied. In fact, we argue in Error #7 (failure to establish training criteria) that in the majority of bare bones studies learning cannot be clearly demonstrated. Learning is not demonstrated by a few mmHg change in blood pressure (Elder and Eustis, 1975; Surwit, Shapiro, and Good, 1978); a few b.p.m. in heart rate (Bouchard and Granger, 1977; Schwartz, 1972); a two or three degree increase in hand temperature (Achterberg, McGraw, and Lawlis, 1981; Gamble and Elder, 1983; Guglielmi et al., 1982; Stoffer et al., 1979,) and small changes in muscle tension (O'Connell and Yeaton, 1981; Phillips, 1977; Weinman, et al., 1983).

When it became clear that bare bones biofeedback was likely to fail, some researchers began using instructions and found that instructions do improve learning, (Bergman & Johnson, 1971; Bouchard & Granger, 1978; Herzfeld & Taub, 1980; Hoon, 1980; Lacroix & Roberts, 1978; Stephens, Harris, & Brady, 1972). If this seemed surprising it was because biofeedback was thought to be so powerful that mere exposure to the machine could change behavior.

The research on the use of cognitive behavior modification in sports psychology and psychotherapy has demonstrated the importance of positive instructions, positive self-talk, and positive imagery for effective coaching, teaching and therapy with humans (Cox, 1985; Heil, 1984; Lazarus, 1975; Meichenbaum, 1976; Mickelson & Stevic, 1971; Shaw & Blanchard, 1983; Suinn, 1984; Weinberg, 1984). In addition, research in psychology, sports and education over the past 30 years has demonstrated the importance of a positive interaction between teacher and student, coach and athlete, therapist and client (Aspy, 1969; Carkhuff & Berenson,

1976; Cox, 1985; Kratochvil, Carkhuff, & Berenson, 1969; Smoll & Smith, 1984; Taub, 1977; Truax & Mitchell, 1971).

The importance of the positive or negative expectations of the coach or teacher on motivation and performance has been well documented (Brawley & Roberts, 1984; Cox, 1985; Horn, 1984; Martinek, 1981). Motivation and performance can be enhanced by the coach, teacher or therapist, and are relevant in biofeedback training research, just as they are in biofeedback training, but have rarely been recognized due to the category mistakes of the ghost in the box. In fact, these variables have been excluded in ghost in the box methodology because researchers believe that they contaminate the results, making the specific drug-like effect of biofeedback difficult to detect. ". . . rather, the evidence for informational biofeedback's efficacy has to be in the form of control conditions that show that an appreciable amount of increased control can indeed be attributed to the information supplied and not to the placebo-related effects such as motivation, self-instruction, relaxation and subject selection" (Furedy, 1979, p. 206).

When a coaching model is employed, biofeedback training includes an appropriate rationale and instructions, a variety of psychophysiological training techniques, motivation enhancement, and home practice with or without a home biofeedback unit. With this methodology the maximum potential of biofeedback training to facilitate learning and psychophysiological change is studied.

As learning is facilitated by departing from bare bones trial-and-error methodology, studies show greater learning as described in Chapter 4, Successful Biofeedback Training. This is true in clinical practice as well.

Methodology Error #6: **Double-blind designs.**
Conceptual Error: **The biofeedback box and signals coming from it are so powerful that the trainer and trainee can be "blind" to the goals, methods, and relevant feedback for successful training and symptom reduction (Category Mistake #1).**

The double-blind design used in biofeedback training research is the quintessential example of Category Mistake #1 and its consequences. In this case a design appropriate to the study of the effect of chemicals on physiology is used to study the effect of biofeedback on physiology. The essence of the biofeedback mirror is to remove blindfolds and provide salient information for learning. The essence of the double-blind design as used by Furedy (1985), Guglielmi et al. (1982), Kewman and Roberts (1980), Whitset, Lubar, Holder, Pomplin, and Shabsin (1982) is to "blindfold" the trainer and trainee to the salient feedback of information. In these studies subjects are given signals from a biofeedback machine that reflect a physiological process, but are not informed of the contingency. For example, Guglielmi et al. (1982) attached a thermister and EMG electrodes to each Raynaud's patient, but to keep the subjects "blinded" they were not told which physiological process was creating the feedback. "They all received both auditory and visual feedback, but they were not told about the nature of direction of the physiological change upon which feedback was contingent. They were simply instructed to "drive" the feedback meter and tone in one direction" (p. 107). Why these researchers refer to this process as "training" is unclear.

Double-blind studies of this type cannot measure the effectiveness of biofeedback training, because they are not biofeedback studies. What is being studied? The ghost in the box that is not there. Using this type of double-blind design in biofeedback training research is like putting a blindfolded person in front of a mirror to determine whether or not the mirror has a specific effect. When the double-blind design produces little learning and symptom reduction, researchers inevitably conclude that biofeedback was not effective. "The results of the present investigation clearly indicate that the best treatment for Raynaud's Disease is warm weather" (Guglielmi, et al., 1982, p. 118.). This is like concluding that because a blindfolded person has difficulty learning to braid her hair while standing in front of a mirror, the mirror is not effective. The conclusion is false and so it is in biofeedback research.

With this type of double-blind design, direct comparisons are made between exposure to signals from a biofeedback instrument and symptoms, by-passing the essential ingredient, learning; the comparison of the training effect (the degree of learning) to the treatment effect (the degree of symptom reduction) is missed (Fahrion, 1978).

Because learning is irrelevant to the effect of drugs on symptoms, when the double-blind design is applied to biofeedback training two consequences may occur: (a) the design itself hinders learning by eliminating much that goes with learning: appropriate goals, appropriate feedback, coaching, adjunctive tools, appropriate homework instructions, and motivation that arises from success and knowledge, and (b) the researcher fails *a priori* to appreciate the role of learning (as distinct from mere physiological change) in symptom reduction. Double-blind methodology of the Guglielmi et al. variety necessarily implies that biofeedback training does not involve learning, that biofeedback has a special power independent of the user and provider, as do drugs. This implication and the research that followed from it have hindered the development of biofeedback training and falsely underestimated its potential.

The Kewman and Roberts double-blind study (1980) with migraine patients deserves mention here although it has been well critiqued by Steiner and Dince (1981). In this study migraineurs received feedback for either increases or decreases in hand temperature; subjects were of course not aware of the contingency. As in the later study by Guglielmi et al. (1982), this "blindness" is justified by the fact that rats can learn and they seem to be unconscious of the target response. The human data however, indicate the contrary. Subjects failed to learn to increase or decrease hand temperature, contradicting the authors claim that learning occurred. "Learning" to increase hand temperature is defined as a temperature change from 87.2°F to 88.5°F (group means), and "learning" to decrease is defined as a temperature change from 88.8°F to 87.6°F (group means), all within normal variation (Error #10, failure to establish reliability). Subjects with less change were termed "non-learners." Kewman and Roberts seem to be unconcerned by the fact that some subjects receiving feedback for decreases in temperature were later assigned to the "learned increase" group because their temperatures went up, and vice versa. This is not learning, this is quasi-random variation in hand temperature. But because Kewman and Roberts choose to call a slight variation "learning," they can claim that learning to decrease hand temperature is as effective as learning to increase hand temperature in reducing symptomology since these groups had somewhat similar treatment results. Phrases used by these authors such as "migraine patients who learned to raise finger temperature," ". . .those trained to lower finger temperature," and "learning criterion" are psychophysiologically and scientifically incorrect and misleading. This misuse of the term "learning" is discussed further in Error #7, failure to establish training criteria.

The studies referenced above are actually not "double-blind" studies as used in drug research because no group was given the "active ingredient" i.e. true, contingent feedback of information that could be used for learning. Other double-blind studies have included a feedback training group, but because researchers using the double-blind design have accepted the drug model, training in the feedback group is minimal. Hatch et al. (1983) included a contingent feedback group in their double-blind study on EMG training with normal subjects, but in this single session study, subjects in the feedback, false feedback and pseudofeedback groups were given one instruction, ". . . reach the deepest level of relaxation." Other than this, trial-and-error learning was the only strategy available to the feedback group. It is not surprising that the contingent and noncontingent groups had similar results.

Furthermore, even in "correct" double-blind studies, the trainer is blind, and doesn't know whether or not the trainee is receiving contingent or false feedback. Again, training is minimal because effective coaching is prevented.

The assumptions that biofeedback instruments have a special power to change behavior, and that learning is not essential for this power to have its effect are also tacitly incorporated in the ABA' design (treatment-no-treatment-treatment or baseline-treatment-baseline) advocated and used by many researchers (Blanchard & Young, 1974). This design suggests that when the subject is exposed to biofeedback in the A phase behavior will change, and when the feedback is removed or falsified, phase B, the conditioned behavior will extinguish. To be sure, if the effectiveness of a medication such as an anticonvulsant or insulin is studied the loss of the behavior in the B phase is expected. (The loss of behavior is not expected if the medication is administered to facilitate a cure, however.) A problem with the ABA' design is described by Whitsett et al. (1982), in their report of a double-blind study on EEG and seizure activity:

> An additional complication stemmed from the ABA design that was incorporated. Although this particular paradigm was utilized to strengthen the claim of operant control over the EEG, and to rule out placebo and other nonspecific effects, it may have made acquisition of the task too difficult for several patients. The reversal of contingencies during the B phase, in particular, appeared to cause considerable distress for some patients, despite the fact that the patients were not informed of the change (p. 207).

(It is curious that while this type of design is used to rule out the positive placebo effect, the possibility that a negative placebo effect might seriously affect results is not considered.)

Sterman (1985) reported a situation similar to that of Whitsett et al. (1982) in an SMR study in which a subject knew when the B phase was initiated. In essence the subject's attitude was: "I know exactly what I am doing and I am not going to produce a brain wave that is not effective." In this case the subject had apparently become aware of the subjective correlates of SMR and had gained mastery of the rhythm, certainly the goal of biofeedback training.

These designs may be appropriate if the treatment being studied necessitates neither consciousness nor learning on the part of the subject. These conditions are not true of successful biofeedback training. In successful biofeedback training consciousness and learning are fundamental.

To a clinician, the ABA' and similar designs are problematic. Ideally, if the clinician and the patient have done their jobs well, there is no substantial decrement of behavior with termination of treatment (A' or B phase, depending on the design); the behavior has been learned and brought under conscious control and should be independent of the training tool and trainer. Cessation of treatment is a test of treatment success; extinction is not expected, and further improvement at follow-up would not be surprising. By analogy, after the child has learned to say the alphabet in kindergarten this behavior should be maintained during withdrawal of treatment called summer vacation. If the child loses the behavior over the summer months the teacher might be dismissed. If the child practices the alphabet over the summer months, improvement in alphabet-saying is expected. The double-blind, and ABA' designs illustrate the self-fulfilling prophecy—conditions are created in which learning cannot occur and "biofeedback" must fail, and indeed it does.

These designs are inappropriately applied to biofeedback training, and the results generated from them have hindered the development of the field and its acceptance as a treatment modality.

Methodology Error #7: **Failure to establish training criteria.** *Conceptual Error:* Criteria for determining successful training are not needed. A training effect is not necessary since the power is in the machine (Category Mistakes #1 and #2).

Failure to establish performance goals arises naturally from Category Mistakes #1 and #2. Had researchers not been so mystified by the assumed drug-like power of the biofeedback machine, long ago they would have asked "To what level should subjects and patients train?" As an example many studies on the effectiveness of biofeedback training for remediation of tension or migraine headache failed to establish training goals. Furthermore, the authors do not report training results but simply report treatment results (Chesney & Shelton, 1976; Cox, Freundlich & Meyer, 1975; Diamond, Medina, Diamond-Falk, & Deveno, 1979; Fried et al., 1977; Haynes, Giffin, Mooney, & Parise,1975; McKenzie, Ehrisman, Montgomery & Barnes, 1974; Medina, Diamond, and Franklin, 1976; Sturgis et al., 1978). Apparently learning data are not reported because learning is not thought to be the essential variable; "biofeedback" is the essential variable, meaning exposure to signals from the biofeedback instrument.

Failure to establish training criteria and train patients to these criteria encompasses another error—failure to appreciate the essential link between training and treatment, (and the need to study this link), currently referred to as the training effect (degree of learning) vs. the treatment effect (degree of symptom reduction), (Blanchard, et al., 1980; Fahrion, 1978; Libo, 1983b; Steiner & Dince, 1981 and 1983). While successful training by the patient has not occurred in many studies, it is nonetheless expected that significant changes in symptomatology should result—that the "treatment effect" is somehow independent of the "training effect." In *A Biofeedback Primer* (1978) Blanchard and Epstein write:

> One report (Kaplan) has *failed to confirm the efficacy of SMR [sensorimotor rhythm] feedback training for the treatment of epilepsy* [emphasis added]. Kaplan treated two epileptics for three months with feedback of the

SMR. Neither showed any improvement in seizure rate or *any evidence of learning to produce SMR* [emphasis added] although a technique similar to Sterman's was used. Her systematic case studies thus throw some doubt on Sterman's procedure (p. 143).

Although Kaplan's subjects failed to learn to produce SMR, Blanchard and Epstein conclude that her study fails to confirm the efficacy of SMR feedback for seizure reduction, and suggest that this casts doubt on Sterman's procedure. They can *only* conclude that SMR is difficult to learn. Obviously Kaplan's study says nothing about the efficacy of SMR feedback training. In fact, it is doubtful that this could be called an SMR feedback study. In order to receive SMR feedback, subjects must be learning to produce the brainwave rhythm (unlike other continuous physiological variables such as temperature, or muscle tension). These authors, and others, make this type of error because they believe that training and treatment effects are not related. In this case, Blanchard and Epstein apparently believe that if the procedure is effective, then by merely being connected to the SMR feedback device epileptics should experience seizure reduction independently of learning—again, the ghost in the box mythology.

It was for good reasons that early pioneers in biofeedback training emphasized the fact that criteria to demonstrate significant learning must be established before making claims about the treatment effect, or before correlating the treatment effect with biofeedback training, (Budzynski, et al., 1977; Fahrion, 1978). It is curious that this simple logic has been missed.

Due to the mythology of the ghost in the box, these early researchers were not heeded. The irony is that on this issue, if official doctrine researchers had been truer to the drug model they would have investigated the "dosage" necessary to achieve the desired treatment effect. Blanchard, Andrasik and Silver (1980) argue against training to criterion while still justifying their conclusion that biofeedback is not effective in the treatment of muscle contraction headache. "Another criticism leveled by Belar is that no studies utilized a learning to criterion as part of the biofeedback training. While this is a valid observation, there is no evidence that this would be an effective strategy" (p. 22). The circularity of this reasoning is striking. The fact that these studies lacked training criteria is not evidence from which to conclude that criteria are not needed. This is a misuse of the category "no evidence." In scientific investigation it is concluded that there is no evidence for the effect of the experimental variable only after having carefully studied the variable and not before. This type of equivocation with the term "no evidence" is used repeatedly by Kewman and Roberts (1983).

Many clinicians and researchers have found that when patients fail to achieve generalized low arousal states minimal treatment results occur, and when patients achieve generalized low arousal states, maximal treatment results occur. Libo and Arnold (1983) in a 1 to 5 year follow-up study of 49 patients found that all patients who achieved training criteria on both EMG (1 μV RMS) and finger temperature (95°F) reported long-term improvement, (N = 12). Of the patients who did not improve (N = 11), eight had not achieved training criterion in either modality. It was found that of the 26 remaining patients who achieved criterion on one modality only, 23 showed long term improvement. Similar data are reported by Fahrion, Norris, Green, and Green (1986) on EMG and temperature training for blood pressure reduction, and by Budzynski et al., (1973).

In spite of their earlier viewpoint, Blanchard, Andrasik, and associates have begun to examine the relation between the training and the treatment effect (Acerra, Andrasik, & Blanchard, 1984). A preliminary result from their work with essential hypertensives is: "Repeated measures ANOVA revealed that those patients who were able to raise their hand temperature to at least 97°F during biofeedback showed decreases in diastolic blood pressure from one week pre-treatment to the last week of treatment (p = .001)." They conclude: "The home blood pressure data supports the idea of a relationship between reaching a criterion and clinical outcome" (p. 5).

If the necessity to train to criterion were recognized, it would not be acceptable for grant writers and graduate students to propose that subjects be trained for a predetermined number of sessions rather than to a particular level of performance or symptom reduction. Typically grant proposals state the number of sessions to be given; when that number is reached the experiment ends, whether or not the trainees have learned self regulation of the variable being studied, or symptoms are reduced. If symptoms are not reduced beyond the control group, conclusions are negative. A more scientific approach would be to train patients to a point of substantial symptom reduction and then through an analysis of the training data determine the necessary criteria for training, for particular symptoms. Or, adequately train subjects in self regulation skills, and only then draw conclusions about the efficacy of biofeedback training for symptom reduction.

Failure to establish criteria with which to determine learning has led to another serious problem—every researcher has a different definition of "learning." In many reports "learning" is assumed if any change occurs in the variable being studied, as seen in the Kewman and Roberts double-blind migraine study described above. Onoda (1983) conducted a study in which one group of subjects was instructed to relax and warm their hands, and one group was instructed to relax and cool their hands; eight one-half hour sessions were given. Onoda concludes:

> Since there was no significant difference in reported subjective relaxation between the WR [warm-relax] and CR [cool-relax] groups, a clear pattern between physiological change in hand temperature and subjective relaxation cannot be established. These findings suggest that the use of hand-warming with a "normal" population to enhance relaxation is largely placebo, or due to nonspecific effects (p. 113).

In examining the temperature data it is clear that no learning occurred. The mean decrease over eight sessions for the cool group was 1.7°F and appears to vary randomly; the mean increase for the warm group was 3.38°F and temperature gains actually decreased in the last three sessions, ending with a mere 1.4°F increase in the final session. This is not learning. Why the author expected that subjective cues could be attached to these small variations in temperature is unclear, (unfortunately absolute measurements are not given). Naturally these groups have similiar subjective experience since neither learned to control the response and both were told to relax. This study does not contribute to our knowledge of the subjective experiences of hand warming and cooling.

In the Stoffer et al. study (1979) an increase in temperature of at least 0.3º C was considered significant; no differences were found between the feedback group, yoked control and no-treatment groups. Unlike many studies the authors did include a demonstration of "learning" task, and in this task the feedback group did exceed the control groups. The magnitude of increase during the demonstration of voluntary control however, was "typically less that 0.5º C" (p.59). In spite of minimal learning (it is suggested that small changes may have been due to high baseline temperatures) results on a cold pressor test led the authors to conclude: "There is no indication that previous temperature training influenced blood pressure, heart rate, subjective pain, or immersion time during the cold pressor test given under no-feedback conditions. Stress modulation effects of training may not apply to temperature control" (p. 59). As noted in the previous error, the use of phrases such as "learning" and "control" in studies of this type are both inaccurate and misleading.

Unfounded conclusions such as these occur because there are no well established criteria for learning among researchers. Were adequate criteria established, these studies would have been conducted differently, or would not have been published with faulty conclusions.

In Chapter Four, Successful Biofeedback Training, we discuss the relationship between training to criteria and successful outcomes.

Methodology Error #8 : Using a relaxation control group for comparison to biofeedback training.
Conceptual Error: Relaxation training and biofeedback training are different; biofeedback has power independently of relaxation (Category Mistake #1).

Kewman and Roberts (1983) state: "There is uncertainty as to whether the efficacy of biofeedback exceeds that of relaxation training alone" (p. 489). Chesney and Shelton (1976) write: "Relaxation training and practice rather than biofeedback are essential in the treatment of muscle contraction headaches" (p. 225). Price states: "One primary defect is that biofeedback has generally not been found to be superior to training in relaxation only" (Price, 1979, p. 146). "Unfortunately, these sustained improvements [in blood pressure] cannot be attributed to the effects of biofeedback training alone since general relaxation training was incorporated into the treatment procedures as well" (Yates, 1980. p.491). Searching for the specific effect of biofeedback and not finding it, Beatty writes: "Furthermore, detailed studies of the hemodynamic effects of hand-warming procedures suggest that any observed therapeutic effect cannot be attributed to specific effects on the pathophysiological processes, but rather are indicative of generalized relaxation." Thus Beatty concludes ". . . these data speak quite clearly against the continued use of biofeedback procedures in the treatment of migraine . . ." (Beatty, 1982, p. 220). In numerous studies the experimental and control groups are described as follows: the experimental group received biofeedback training and the control group received relaxation training, (Alexander, 1975; Cox et al., 1975; Coursey, 1975; Haynes, Mosley, & McGowan, 1975). In many cases a specific type of relaxation training is compared to biofeedback training. What is meant by biofeedback training?

The belief in a specific drug-like power of biofeedback led to the methodological concern that any relaxation technique used in conjunction with the feedback would confound the results. "Blanchard and Young were forced to conclude that while the data looked promising, the unique contribution of EMG feedback had been consistently confounded with both the inclusion of other relaxation methods during training and regular home practice of nonfeedback relaxation" (Alexander & Smith, 1979, p. 124). By analogy, this is to suggest that we could and should study the unique contribution of the mirror to behavior, for example hairbrushing, without the additional aid of a brush.

When trainees learn to increase blood flow in their hands or lower muscle tension they are learning to relax. This fact is not clear to many researchers who seem to believe that biofeedback has a specific drug-like effect that increases hand temperature or reduces EMG level or decelerates the heart, independently of relaxation. *But there is nothing inherently relaxing about the feedback of information, and feedback is not a relaxation procedure* any more than the reflection in the mirror is a procedure. Biofeedback information merely aids in the learning of relaxation.

To achieve the goal of increased blood flow in the hands or lower muscle tension, relaxation must be learned by whatever methods are effective. These methods can be either *unsystematic* or *systematic*. When researchers believe that biofeedback has a specific effect and instructions and coaching should not be given, then the only learning method with which the trainee can learn relaxation (hand warming or lowering EMG, or heart rate reduction) is trial-and-error, an unsystematic and often ineffective approach. When it is understood that the feedback of information is merely an aid to learning, then the goal of increased blood flow in the hands or reduced muscle tension is taught through a variety of systematic relaxation techniques such as autogenic training, progressive relaxation, breathing techniques and imagery techniques. Studies that compare a "biofeedback" group to a relaxation control group are usually comparing trial-and-error learning, to learning a systematic relaxation technique, (or simply the instruction to relax), not a useful comparison and certainly misleading.

The extent to which the subject learns to voluntarily create the subjective experience and achieve the physiological parameters of relaxation, is the extent to which hand warming or muscle tension reduction will be learned; feedback of information aids in that process but is not a relaxation technique in itself. *Because relaxation (low arousal) is the psychophysiological process that brings the body back to healthy homeostasis*, it is no surprise that the relaxation group does better than the biofeedback group in achieving low arousal and symptom reduction in these studies. Whatever the biofeedback group is doing, it apparently is not relaxation, other than that gained by trial-and-error attempts at changing the feedback. In addition, subjects in a relaxation control group, without feedback, undoubtedly initiate "passive volition." In contrast, subjects given feedback and a task to perform, may use "active volition" in attempts to succeed, a counterproductive strategy in learning psychophysiological control in most cases.

This misleading confusion of "biofeedback" and "relaxation" contributes also to the issue of homework. If biofeedback were considered to be a tool for enhancing relaxation skills, or relaxation skills useful for enhancing biofeedback training, the usefulness of homework exercises would be clear. Certainly biofeedback training subjects/patients could practice relaxation at home without a biofeedback instrument, and thus enhance their relaxation skills, probably beyond that of the control "relaxation" group since the feedback group would have feedback in the laboratory to confirm the efficacy of their relaxation strategies. When the biofeedack group is given relaxation strategies and home training, the biofeedback group is found to be superior to a relaxation control group (Blanchard et al.,1982a; Blanchard et al., 1982b). When the power is thought to be in the instrument which is generally not sent home (early exceptions are Budzynski et al., 1973; Sargent, Green, & Walters, 1973; and Sterman, 1977), and when biofeedback training is thought to be something different from relaxation training, the need for homework is not appreciated. Subjects and patients are denied an important aspect of training.

The early article by Stoyva and Budzynski (1974) emphasizing the need for generalized low arousal measured on several modalities, (temperature, GSR, forearm EMG, and forehead EMG) has been essentially disregarded in research until recently. Stoyva and Budzynski noted that the crucial issue is self regulation of the low arousal states of deep relaxation, and the initial goal of training is generalized low arousal by whatever method(s) the patient finds most efficacious. In clinical practice we do not attempt to treat the patient with only one training method or feedback modality. Several techniques and modalities are used and the patient determines which is most beneficial (the locus of control is purposefully internal). In our clinical work and research (Shellenberger, Turner,

Green, and Cooney, 1986, and Shellenberger et al., 1983), we find that subjects and patients prefer a variety of systematic relaxation techniques and biofeedback modalities.

Failure to appreciate the value of generalized low arousal (Category Mistake #1—biofeedback has the power to create change independently of the internal state of the patient), has resulted in poor research results. Fahrion, et al., (1986) argues that many blood pressure studies have produced minimal results because a state of generalized low arousal was not achieved by subjects. Furthermore, when generalized low arousal is the goal, the issue of specificity between feedback modality and symptom is irrelevent. We raise the issue of specificity here because it has a bearing on the issue of relaxation versus biofeedback. If it is assumed that a specific illness should be treated with a specific biofeedback modality or relaxation technique, and that biofeedback and relaxation are different, then the risk of minimal biofeedback training and poor results is imminent.

In summary, there are three options for understanding biofeedback and relaxation training:

(1) Feedback of information is an aid to unsystematic relaxation training—trial-and-error feedback learning;

(2) Feedback of information is an aid to systematic relaxation training: autogenic feedback training (Green, Green, & Walters, 1970), progressive feedback training (Budzynski, 1973a), open focus feedback training (Fritz, 1985), and quieting response feedback training (Ford, Stroebel, Strong, & Szarek, 1983).

(3) Feedback of information is not an aid to unsystematic or systematic training but has a specific effect of its own—the ghost in the box.

Methodology Error #9: **Failure to incorporate mental/emotional variables in biofeedback training.**
Conceptual Error: **Biofeedback has a power of its own independent of the user; the conscious mind does not play a significant role in biofeedback (Category Mistakes #1 and #2).**

This conceptual error is the fundamental presupposition for the category mistakes, and of the conceptual and methodological errors described above. By "mind" we mean that uniquely human complex of emotions, expectations, self-talk, visualizations, goals, volition, private agendas, perceptions, beliefs, attitudes, language and consciousness. Not of great importance in drug and animal research, these variables have been neglected in human research. Had these human variables been acknowledged, facilitated and employed in biofeedback research, the field might have advanced rapidly in the first decade.

Understanding the category mistakes enables us to understand the contention that consciousness is not necessary for successful biofeedback training. In spite of the failure of their research to achieve either a training effect or a treatment effect, Guglielmi, Roberts and Patterson (1982) nevertheless argue this point: "Furthermore, in recent years a body of literature has accumulated indicating that what is true for rats also applies to humans [knowledge of the feedback-relevant response is not necessary]" (p. 117). To support this contention they quote from a Biofeedback Society of America task force report ". . . There appears to be no basis for the claim by many clinicians that awareness of the feedback-relevant response is necessary in order to achieve self-control over the response . . . In fact, the weight of the evidence to date indicates that nonawareness produces results equal to or better than awareness" (Carlson, 1978, p.7). The few studies that led to this conclusion contain so many methodological errors, including Error #11 (lack of reliability measures) and contradictions (the use of the term "self-control" when self control was never achieved), that this puzzling claim is easily understood. It is possible to so befuddle the feedback group that knowledge of the response is of no benefit whatsoever. In fact physiological change may be the opposite of that intended, indicating arousal or confusion.

Here is a fascinating paradox: on one hand, biofeedback research of the "official doctrine" type has failed to acknowledge and investigate the powerful impact of mind on body (to discover for example, which particular cognitions facilitate physiological change and symptom reduction), while on the other hand, it has wholeheartedly attempted to eliminate this impact by calling it the "placebo effect." This is inconsistent. Verbally and conceptually, researchers deny the existence or power of the conscious mind, and yet confirm the existence and power of the mind by insisting on rigorous research to control for the placebo effect—the mind's power to influence physiology through belief.

The double-blind design applied to "self-regulation" research is an excellent example of this paradox and the magical thinking about biofeedback. The mind is considered powerful but contaminating and is therefore "removed" from the treatment, or at least "controlled for" in the research design. It is hoped that by systematically controlling for all the cognitive and situational variables that might contaminate the results, at last the pure effect of "biofeedback" will be demonstrated. It is erroneous to assume that biofeedback has a drug-like power that when purified and dispensed in given doses may yield "pure" results. When this is attempted, the magical power seems to fail. This is because it was never there in the first place. Using a drug analogy, "biofeedback" fails because so many of the powerful ingredients are removed, ingredients that interact synergistically with the pure feedback of information to facilitate training.

The uniqueness of biofeedback training is that the user of the information, the trainee, produces the physiological information in the first place, in the same way that the user of the mirror produces the information that is reflected in the mirror. Therefore anything that affects the user affects the feedback. Because the information from the instrument is often research data, anything that affects the user affects the data. A continuous synergistic loop exists between the user's cognitive processing, the impact of cognitions on the user's physiology, and the feedback information, or data. Any variable that affects one of these components alters the entire process. Many biofeedback researchers have not considered this fact other than to control for the placebo effect. In general, researchers have neither used the impact of cognitions on physiology to the subjects benefit, nor considered the effect on the data that negative cognitions might have. Donald Meichenbaum (1976) states:

> ... It is proposed that the biofeedback literature to date could be compared to the verbal-conditioning literature prior to the active research on the role of awareness in the conditioning process. The research on awareness (e.g., Dulany, 1962; Spielberger & Denike, 1966) questioned whether the experimenter's reinforcement acted in an automatic fashion and it highlighted the important role of the client's knowledge of the reinforcement contingencies and his motivation to comply. The biofeedback literature requires as much similar attention to the client's cognitive processes. Such attention to the client's cognitive process at each phase of the biofeedback training should result in the training becoming more effective and will help elucidate the mechanisms that contribute to change (p. 216).

Meichenbaum, in this article, and Lazarus (1975), have been unheeded. The cognitions of the subject or patient in biofeedback research have been viewed as confounding variables, and have not been elicited or regarded as meaningful data. Engel (1972) writes ". . . it is small wonder that I have not been able to find any consistency among the stories that patients have told me. I am certain that they do not know what they are doing, and that they are just making up stories to please me" (p. 205). Undoubtedly this bias against subject reports arises from the belief in the ghost in the box and from the belief that such reports are unscientific, and from the methodologies of the operant conditioning model that disallow an appreciation or enhancement of *individual learning styles*. If subject reports had been elicited and used to enhance training, biofeedback research might have kept pace with its clinical applications.

Many researchers have believed that the effect of the feedback information can be isolated and studied separately from the human mind using the information. "Rather, the evidence for informational biofeedback's efficacy has to be in the form of control conditions that show that an appreciable amount of increased control can indeed be attributed to the information supplied and not to other placebo-related effects such as motivation, self-instruction, relaxation and subject selection'' (Furedy, 1979, p. 206). This is an impossible task—as impossible as trying to study the characteristics of water by isolating and studying the characteristics of hydrogen. Like hydrogen and oxygen that combine to create water, information feedback and the conscious mind using the information combine in an interactive process called biofeedback training.

Methodology Error #10: **Failure to establish reliability measures and confidence bands.**
Conceptual Error: **Psychophysiological parameters in humans are invariant thus reliability studies are not needed (Category Mistake #1).**

In 1982, we hired a researcher, John Cooney, Ph.D., not in the field of biofeedback, to help us assess the effectiveness of our biofeedback and stress management programs (Shellenberger et al., 1986). The first task he proposed was to examine the reliability of our measures. Before doing this we searched the literature for reliability studies on EDR, EMG, and thermal measures. To our surprise, we could not find a single article in the major journals on reliability. As a result, we found it necessary to examine reliability coefficients for two different groups (Shellenberger, Green, Cooney, & Turner, 1983). One group (N = 85) was a no-treatment control group that was given a stress profile using EMG, EDR, and thermal measures on day 1 and day 60. A second group (N = 149) was given the same stress profile before and after a ten week course on biofeedback training and stress management.

Simultaneously, the Stress Disorders Clinic at the State University of New York was conducting a reliability study with 15 subjects in which EMG, EDR, thermal, and heart rate measures were recorded on days 1, 2, 14, and 28 (Arena, Blanchard, Andrasik, Cotch, & Myers, 1983).

The conclusions of the two studies were similar: EMG was the only measure that was somewhat reliable. Arena et al. conclude:

> The results of the present study contain a straight-forward message for the majority of research involving psychophsyiological measurements: investigators must first ascertain how reliable are these measures on their respective subject population and then employ in their research only those measures which are found to be reliable on their populations (p. 458).

The authors of this important study make another point:

> Traditionally behavioral assessment has emphasized situational specificity as opposed to stable trait-like characteristics of individuals (Goldfried and Kent, 1972). It seems unusual then that behaviorally-oriented researchers and clinicians would assume that psychophysiological measures are relatively stable over time. Unfortunately, this assumption seems to have been the case; with but one exception (Sturgis, 1980), behavioral investigators have in recent years not concerned themselves with issues of reliability of this class of measures (p. 443).

The failure to determine the reliablilty of psychophysiological measures in humans arises primarily from an assumption implicit in Category Mistake #2—human physiology is as invariant as laboratory animal physiology. The physiology of the caged animal is assumed to be minimally affected by situational conditions and not affected at all by "cognitive" variables. The unstated assumption is that human physiology is the same and ticks away day after day, invariant unless manipulated by an external power such as biofeedback or drugs. It is implicitly assumed that reliability studies against which to measure the impact of the treatment are not necessary.

Human physiology, however, is affected by multiple situational and cognitive variables outside the experimenter's control: interpersonal stressors, monetary stressors, diet, exercise habits, drugs, belief systems, expectations, volition. Because these variables affect psychophysiological measures, they affect reliability. As a result, comparing an individual's baseline readings to training readings over several sessions becomes meaningless in the absence of the standard error of measurement.

The purpose of the standard error of measurement is to estimate the stability of measures over time. The standard error of measurement (S_e) given by the formula below requires knowledge of the standard deviation (S) and reliability (r_{xx}) of the measurements.

$$S_e = S \sqrt{1-r_{xx}}$$

Once the S_e for each measurement is obtained, 68% or 95% confidence bands are placed about each data point on a person's initial baseline session. To our knowledge, no standardization of psychophysiological data has included confidence bands. Without norms and confidence bands it becomes difficult to determine whether or not an individual's change from baseline to training sessions is:

(1) a normal fluctuation of psychophysiological states, or
(2) adaptation to the experimental or clinical situation, or
(3) genuine learning, or
(4) clinically significant learning (i.e. the individual has mastered deep levels of relaxation).

To illustrate the problem, it is useful to examine confidence bands based on the most reliable measure, forehead EMG. Figure 1 shows the confidence bands (68%) of forehead EMG measures of a 38 year old healthy male [no symptoms (Cornell Medical Index), normal Minnesota Multiphasic Personality Inventory, and normal State-Trait (STAI)] who participated in the no-treatment control group (mean age for males was 35, SD 4.8)

These confidence bands show a tremendous variability in the subject's physiology. The group standard deviation at baseline of 8.7 μV peak-to-peak and the reliabilty coefficient of .52 accounts for the large variability.

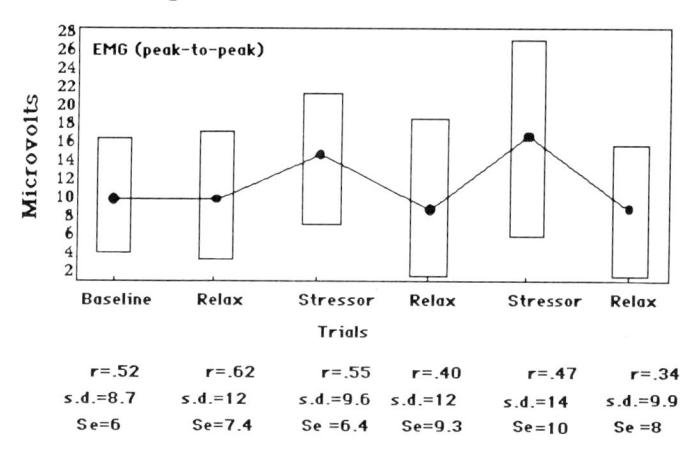

Figure 1: EMG Confidence Bands

	Baseline	Relax	Stressor	Relax	Stressor	Relax
	r=.52	r=.62	r=.55	r=.40	r=.47	r=.34
	s.d.=8.7	s.d.=12	s.d.=9.6	s.d.=12	s.d.=14	s.d.=9.9
	Se=6	Se=7.4	Se=6.4	Se=9.3	Se=10	Se=8

In an attempt to improve our reliability measures and achieve the .80 reliability coefficient standard set by the American Psychological Association (1974), and to narrow the confidence bands, we replicated the reliability study of the Stress Disorders

Clinic (Arena, et. al, 1983). In our replication study (Shellenberger and Lewis, 1986), physiologic meaures on days 1, 2, 14, and 28 under stressed and relaxed conditions were recorded from 15 healthy subjects. No feedback or training was given. In addition, an attempt was made to regulate and control for many factors that might influence the reliability of the results—diet, drugs, smoking, medications, exercise, stress, humidity and temperature of the testing room, posture during testing, adaptation period, time of day, time of week, emotional state, illness, skin preparation on hands and forehead, electrode impedance, equipment calibration, eyes open/closed, and menstrual cycle. The results were disappointing. Baseline correlations between day 1 and day 28 were .14 for EDR, .16 for hand temperature, and .52 for forehead EMG. One reason for the low correlations was the large adaptation effect that many individuals demonstrated (discussed in Error #11).

The difficulties discussed above are also characteristic of research on other aspects of physiological functioning. For example, John Cohen (1985) in his article, "Stress and the Human Immune Response: A Critical Review," points out that many research studies show a statistically significant difference between control and experimental groups but the differences are too small to be of biological significance. " 'Statistically, but not biologically significant' is a phrase immunologists love to use" (p. 168). Cohen states: "In most laboratories the day-to-day and subject-to-subject variation in mitogen response is such that the range of normal is very wide" (p. 172). This wide range of normal is characteristic of biofeedback measures as well. Differences between control and experimental groups that are found to be significant may fall within the normal variation.

In an excellent methodology article, Banderia et al.(1982), makes a similar criticism of heart rate biofeedback studies and points out that one study obtained a statistically significant heart rate change of .87 beats per minute. This is clearly within the range of normal heart rate variation. Along the same line, Fahrion, Norris, Green, and Green (1986) state, "Most biobehavioral research programs have focused on direct blood pressure feedback which produces statistically significant but not clinically significant effects . . . (p. 18)." Other examples include two microvolt changes or less on EMG measures peak-to-peak (Kinsman, et al., 1975;

O'Connell & Yeaton, 1981; Philips, 1977) and minimal changes in temperature as discussed in Errors #6 and #7. Too often researchers have made claims about the success or failure of biofeedback training on the basis of statistically significant changes in physiological measures without demonstrating the reliability of their measures or demonstrating that a physiologically significant change did or did not occur beyond the range of normal variation. Statistically, but not physiologically significant, aptly describes many biofeedback studies.

Researchers need to establish reliability scores for psychophysiological measures. And, confidence bands and norms need to be established for many variables—sex, age, disease type, level of stress or relaxation, medication status, biofeedback modality, and instrumentation characteristics. This is a difficult task that has not been attempted until recently. In discussion of Error #12 on mastery, we propose a procedure to effectively resolve this problem.

Methodology Error #11: **Failure to control for adaptation.**
Conceptual Error: **Psychophysiologial parameters in humans are invariant (Category Mistake #2).**

The adaptation effect has been well documented and discussed in psychophysiological research, (Kamiya, 1977; Yates, 1980), and while some biofeedback studies have controlled for it, others have not. This error arises from the assumption of invariant measures and/or the assumption of the overwhelming power of biofeedback to create change beyond all other variables.

Data from our reliability studies (Shellenberger and Lewis, 1986, Shellenberger, et al. 1983) indicate that adaptation in some individuals accounts for much of the variance. For example, seven subjects in the repeated profile study exhibited considerable EMG adaptation from Session 1 to Session 4, 28 days later. The mean EMG score for this group in Session 1 was 16.0 microvolts peak-to-peak, and in Session 4 was 8.9 microvolts peak-to-peak, an adaptation change of −7.1 microvolts, indicating relaxation. Seven subjects had a mean temperature increase from 80.5°F in Session 1 to 87.4°F in Session 4, an adaptation increase of 6.9°F, again indicating increased relaxation. These data show across session adaptation.

Equally impressive data indicate within session adaptation. In a normative study in our laboratory (Shellenberger, et al., 1983), of 121 female subjects, (mean age 30.9, SD 11.9, range 17-79), without a 20 minute adaptation period, hand temperature increased from baseline of 78.7°F (SD 7.2) to 84.4°F (SD 8.7) in the first twenty minutes of a standard stress profile. Mean EMG scores for these subjects dropped from 14.5 (SD 8.6) microvolts peak-to-pcak at baseline reading to 9.8 (SD 6.4) microvolts peak-to-peak. In another normative study, Kappes and Morris (1982) found similar results for females (N = 34) on hand temperature. They observed an increase from an initial baseline mean of 84°F to an ending mean of 91°F twenty minutes later. It is clear from these studies that through adaptation alone EMG changes of 7.1 microvolts peak-to-peak or more and temperature increases of 7°F or more may occur within a single session.

It is important to note that the adaptation effect discussed above is the effect of relaxation. It is now clear why studies that have not controlled for adaptation by giving all subjects an extended adaptation period of greater than 20 minutes (*with electrodes attached* in the experimental and control groups) may find that the relaxation or no-treatment control groups show as much or greater change than the biofeedback treatment group.

Studies using a no-treatment control group often require control subjects to sit quietly in the training room for the same period of time as the experimental subjects; physiological change within sessions and between sessions may result. Davis (1980) describes this procedure: "Subjects in the no-treatment condition were instructed to relax as deeply as they could, using any means that was helpful to them" (p. 60). The experimental subjects on the other hand, are immediately subjected to electrode or thermister attachment and feedback, and are given a task to perform, in some cases with no clear idea of how to proceed. Except for the experimental variable, feedback, these groups are assumed to be equal. Clearly these groups are not equal. The no-treatment condition allows adaptation to occur rapidly, while the biofeedback treatment condition may stress the subject and delay both adaptation and learning. When group results are compared, the biofeedback treatment group appears to have done no better than the no-treatment group. Invariably the erroneous conclusion is that biofeedback is not a useful training technique, (Davis, 1980; Nielson & Holmes, 1980; Stoffer, et al., 1979).

The Mastery Model

Methodology Error #12: **Failure to train to mastery.**
Conceptual Error: **Achieving and demonstrating mastery (true self regulation) of the physiological variable being studied is not necessary; the power is in the box (Category Mistake #1).**

Few researchers have developed criteria for training, or advocated training to criteria, and even fewer have trained for psychophysiological self mastery. After many years of research and clinical practice, however, we believe that training for mastery is essential. By mastery we mean the ability to demonstrate the learned skill under adverse conditions, both in and out of the laboratory or clinic. Guidelines for the demonstration of learned skills will be discussed in Chapter 4, Successful Biofeedback Training.

Training to mastery, and the demonstration of mastery are important for many reasons. Stoyva and Budzynski (1974) explicated the first reason by emphasizing that to ensure transfer of skills from laboratory to "real life," stressful situations must be created for the trainee that will simulate real life situations. As a result, Budzynski, Stoyva and Peffer (1977) have done considerable research on determining stressors that will allow the individual to demonstrate self-mastery skills. The need for such training became apparent to Budzynski while working with a patient with elevator phobia (Budzynski, 1977). The patient was given desensitization training with deep relaxation but was unable to control the phobic response when he was unexpectedly confronted with an elevator full of conventioneers. The patient returned to therapy, with the added dimension of training for the worst possible situation, a technique called "flooding." This added ingredient ensured mastery and enabled the patient to transfer the training to all situations. In another case, Miller (1976) trained a patient with hypertension to voluntarily create substantial decreases in diastolic pressure, through extensive training (50 sessions). Miller writes "This patient seemed to be cured because similar decreases were observed on the ward. However, under an unusual combination of emotional stresses, her baseline blood pressure rose, she lost voluntary control, and had to be restored to antihypertensive drugs. After the situational stresses were largely resolved, she returned to training approximately 2.5 years later and has rapidly regained a large measure of voluntary control (Miller, 1976, p. 372). The need for mastery training is clear, that is, the practice and demonstration of the learned skill under adverse conditions as an integral part of training.

Second, mastery reinforces a sense of control in the trainee. The importance of this to successful training cannot be overemphasized. In fact, one study with headache patients (Holroyd, Penzien, Hursey, Tobink, Rogers, Holm, Hall, Marcille, & Chila, 1984) indicates that a sense of control, even if false, may be associated with symptom reduction (subjects were told that they were successfully decreasing forehead EMG when in fact they were being trained to increase EMG).

Third, by gaining mastery based on successful learning patients come to "know that they know" and can maintain and use their skills as needed. Arthur Gladman (1981) who began using biofeedback therapy in his psychiatric practice over fifteen years ago, writes:

> At the moment that the patient becomes aware that he and he alone is changing his symptoms, his concept of himself changes . . . learned deep relaxation and control of a physiologic state in itself produces real change in the physical state and cannot be discounted but, the fact that the individual has developed a sense of mastery, a shift in locus of control, must also be considered in accounting for the remarkable changes that occur in biofeedback training (p. 15).

Mastery facilitates transfer of skills and brings freedom from the feedback equipment and from the therapist.

A fourth reason for demonstrating psychophysiological self mastery is related to the question "How do *we*, the researcher or clinician, know when the trainee has really learned to control a psychophysiological process?" The ability to determine the extent to which the trainee has learned is hindered by (a) the adaptation effect, (b) lack of reliability measures and confidence bands,

(c) wide range of normal variation, (d) the clinical and experimental impracticability of controlling inter- and intrapersonal variables that influence physiology, and (e) dubious inference from group data to the individual (Banderia, et al. 1982). All these problems prevent accurately assessing learning of the experimental or treatment group, and correctly assessing the relationship between psychophysiological training and symptom reduction.

As noted earlier, many researchers have either not attempted to establish a training effect at all, or they have attempted with improper research design to demonstrate learning by (a) comparing baseline scores to training scores without reliability measures or by (b) defining learning as a degree of change in the physiological process being studied that reaches statistical significance, or by (c) defining learning as *any* change in the physiological process.

The most eloquent and practical method for avoiding these difficulties is to *incorporate the demonstration of psychophysiological mastery* into research and clinical practice. This can be done by creating situations in which the trainee can demonstrate self-regulatory abilities, just as we use academic examinations for students to demonstrate learning or competitive events for athletes to demonstrate athletic skill. For example, mastery of blood flow *and the concurrent relaxation response* might be demonstrated by increasing hand temperature on command at a rate of one degree Fahrenheit per minute or greater, in a cold room.

Patients often do demonstrate mastery of psychophysiological variables and stress management skills by handling stressful life events in new ways without exacerbation of symptoms. But in laboratory situations the demonstration of mastery is even more important scientifically because only then can correct conclusions be drawn about the nature of biofeedback training, its potential and its limitations.

If demonstration of mastery is accepted as the *sine qua non* for successful training and for conclusions about biofeedback training, the preceding twelve errors will necessarily be eliminated.

In conclusion, a demonstration of mastery should be incorporated into research and clinical methodology because: (a) It is the only way to know with certainty that the trainee has learned self regulation, particularly when responses are within the normal range of variation (as might be true for successful treatment of a Raynaud's disease patient, for example), and (b) training to mastery is good therapy.

3

Unsuccessful Biofeedback Training

Because so many methodological errors have occurred in the majority of biofeedback studies, it is difficult to determine whether or not biofeedback training has failed. What fails is a methodology based on the mythology of a ghost in the box.

There are many ways to facilitate the failure of biofeedback training. The inclusion of a single error in research design or in clinical practice could induce failure, meaning failure of the trainee to learn, failure in symptom reduction, or failure to establish a connection between training and treatment effects. We wonder why it was expected that learning to regulate a psychophysiological process controlled by the "involuntary" nervous system (and in some cases symptomatic) would be so easy, and the machine so powerful, that all the errors described above would not prevent the experimental group from learning. The answer of course, is that these conceptualizations and methodologies are not considered to be erroneous. Indeed, the category mistakes are blinding.

With these many errors in mind, the puzzling and often contradictory results of many biofeedback training studies can be understood: the control group shows greater change than the biofeedback group; knowledge of the target response hinders learning; statistically significant learning is not associated with symptom reduction; and differences between the no-treatment control group and the experimental feedback group are not significant.

In considering these contradictory findings, questions are automatically raised: What is it that fails? Did the trainee fail?

Did the information fail? Did the experimenter or clinician fail? Did the method fail? Did biofeedback training fail?

Feedback of information cannot fail, nor can it succeed. Just as a mirror neither fails nor succeeds, information feedback is not a phenomenon that can fail or succeed. As discussed above, however, many researchers and reviewers of the field believe that the feedback of information called "biofeedback" can succeed or fail. This has led to confusion in the field of biofeedback training. Because biofeedback training is the *use* of the information by the trainee, in conjunction with systematic training techniques that generate the feedback, there is a *process* that may fail or succeed.

Because so many methodological errors have occurred in the majority of biofeedback studies, it is difficult to determine whether or not biofeedback training has "failed." *What fails is a methodology based on the mythology of a ghost in the box,* a mythology based on category mistakes and false assumptions about the power of feedback and feedback machines. Ancoli and Kamiya (1978), Johansson and Ost (1982) and Thompson, Raczybski, Haber and Sturgis (1983) use different terms but come to similiar conclusions and recommendations in their respective reviews of alpha training studies, biofeedback training studies for migraine headache and studies on muscle contraction headache.

It is important to note that an excellent discussion of research results at the end of a report does not "save" poor methodology and the erroneous conclusions derived from distorted results. Many authors have mentioned these methodological errors in their studies, but do not take them into account in their conclusions. Also, authors reporting poor results repeatedly make reference to other studies with similiar results, attempting to justify their work. Another serious problem for the field of biofeedback training arises from these conclusions. Reviewers of the field seem to read abstracts and conclusions only. From these uncritical reviews the medical and scientific communities are led to believe that research has shown that biofeedback training is not useful or is of minimal use for many disorders (Runck, 1980). In fact most of the biofeedback research literature has not contributed to our ability to assess the efficacy of biofeedback training, in clinical or laboratory settings.

4

Successful Biofeedback Training

Elements of the mastery model have been used from the beginning of biofeedback applications, and it has evolved into a powerful multicomponent approach to psychophysiological self regulation.

When does biofeedback training succeed? The answer depends on how biofeedback training and the goals of biofeedback training are conceptualized.

The goal of official doctrine research is to determine the specific effect of the independent variable: the feedback stimulus, reinforcer, contingency, or information, sometimes called "biofeedback." This goal has resulted in numerous unsuccessful biofeedback studies. Researchers who accurately conceptualize biofeedback as a training process have the *goal of voluntary control of a psychophysiological process for symptom reduction. The independent variable is self regulation.* These researchers understand the essential aspects of biofeedback training, (1) the biofeedback instrument is no more and no less than a mirror—like a mirror, it feeds back information, but has no inherent power to create change in the user; (2) to maximize results, biofeedback training, like any type of complex skill training, involves clear goals, rewards for approximating the goals, enough time and practice for achieving mastery, proper instructions, a variety of systematic training techniques and feedback of information; (3) the person using the feedback must be conscious, must have cognitive understanding of the process and goals, must have positive expectations and positive interaction with the trainer, and must be motivated to learn. Studies based on these ingredients are often successful.

In this chapter, the first task is to examine research studies in which subjects have demonstrated self regulation skills and symptom reduction. The second task is to describe a mastery model of biofeedback training as exemplified in these studies, and in clinical biofeedback practice.

Essential Hypertension and Biofeedback Training (Table 2)

At a time when researchers were abandoning biofeedback for treatment of essential hypertension because their results were statistically, but not clinically significant, Patel (1973 and 1975) achieved statistically and clinically significant results in her work with hypertensive patients.

Schwartz and Shapiro (1973), Surwit and Shapiro (1976), Miller (1975), Elder and Eustis (1975), Fey and Lindholm (1975), and Lutz and Holmes (1981), were trying to isolate a specific effect of blood pressure feedback. Consequently, their methodologies eliminated the essential ingredients for successful biofeedback training. In contrast, Patel's methodology included the essential ingredients for learning successful self regulation and control of essential hypertension, namely, deep levels of general relaxation, home practice, clear instructions and coaching. These are basic elements of a mastery model. Furthermore, Patel used a powerful research design:

> An interesting feature of this study was that 4 months after the completion of a treatment, the subjects in the control condition were given a similar treatment and also showed significant decreases in blood pressure of 28 mm. mercury systolic and 16 mm. mercury diastolic. This use of half cross-over design, in which the untreated controls are now treated and show a response similar to the treated subjects, is a very powerful demonstration of effects because it answers the

possiblity that the treatment effect was specific to the experimental group even with random assignment of subjects. The replication of effects on the controls rules out this possiblity. Follow-up data on these control subjects at 4 months and 7 months showed a maintenance of the gains obtained during treatment (Blanchard, 1979, p. 38).

The work by Patel and her colleagues is summarized in Table 2 with that of other successful studies on essential hypertension.

Table 2
Successful Clinical Biofeedback Training for Essential Hypertension

Study	Treatment	Training Result	Symptom Result
Patel, 1973 Single group outcome N = 20	B: 3 (30 min.) Low arousal training with GSR, autogenic & meditation (36, 30 min. sessions) breathing & relaxing phrases	Avg. decrease in BP: Syst. 25mm Diast: 14mm	12 out of 20 reduced medications; 12 mo. follow-up: Syst. 15mm decrease Diast. 13mm decrease
Patel, 1975 Resting control N = 20; exp. group N = 20	B: 3 session T: same as 1973 study C: 30 min. resting	Avg. decrease in BP: Syst. 20mm Diast. 14mm C Group: Syst. 1mm, Diast. 2mm	12 out of 20 reduced meds.
Patel & North, 1975, E=17, C=17, controlled outcome with crossover.	B:3 sessions T:same (12 sessions)	Avg. decrease in BP: Syst: E=26mm; C=9mm; C after treatment: 28mm Diast: E=15mm; C=4mm; C after treatment: 16mm	

Table 2 continued

Study	Treatment	Training Result	Symptom Result
Patel, Marmot, & Terry, 1981 C=99, E=99	T: deep breathing, deep muscle relaxation, meditation, GSR feedback, stress management training, (8, 60 min. sessions). C: no-treatment control with health education materials.		8 month follow-up showed experimental group significantly lower than control group, 11/8.8mm Hg lower than control group.
Moeller & Love, 1974 Single group outcome, N=6	B: 2 sessions T: forehead EMG & autogenic—17 sessions	Avg. decrease in BP: Syst. 18mm Diast: 12mm	same as training effect
Love, Montgomery, & Moeller, 1974 Control group E=26, C=10.	B:1 session T: 16-32 sessions, forehead EMG & autogenic training	Avg. decrease in BP: Syst: 15mm Diast: 13mm No change in control group	same as training; 8 months follow-up resulted in an additional decrease of 4mm dias. & 6.5mm syst.
Sedlacek, Cohen, 1979 C=10, Benson Relaxation=10, Biofeedback=10	B: 2 yrs. T: 8 sessions of cassette tapes using breathing, relaxation, visual imagery, etc. Thermal & EMG feedback for 12 more sessions training to criteria 90°F & 3 μV (p-p) on forehead, home practice training.	F=reduced from 144/95 to 130/83 (.0001) Relaxation group reduced diastolic (.05) but no change in systolic.	4 month follow-up: T=maintained decrease, 7 reduced medications by 50% or more. Relaxation= 1 reduced meds. C=no change.

Table 2 continued

Study	Treatment	Training Result	Symptom Result
Green, Green, & Norris, 1980. Single group outcome, 9 hypertensives, 6 on medications	T: autogenic feedback training on hands & feet, cognitive training, home practice with temperature machines. B=1 session at intake.	Train to criterion 95°F. + on hands, 90°F. + on feet	6 of 6 at end of training were medication free; other 3 results: 1 subject 139/86 and ended at 118/83; 1 subject 143/94 and ended 145/90 (least amount of training); 1 subject 142/82, ended at 141/79.
Blanchard et al. 1984 Control group outcome to reduce medications E=20, C=20	B: 4 wks home pressures assessment. T: 16 Thermal (20 min.), and autogenic training. C: 8 progressive. Home training for both.	E=13 off 1 drug; C=9 off 1 drug	3 weeks follow-up maintained low pressure even after reduction in medication. Thermal relaxation group showed greater reduction in home blood pressures (.007) than progressive group.
Fahrion, Norris, Green & Green, 1986 Group outcome; 42 patients on medications.	B: 1 week T: Train to criterion of 93°F. on foot, 95.5°F on hands, $3\mu V$ (forehead peak-peak) or below. Sustain criterion levels for 10 min. Treatment included cognitive explanation, breathing exercises, relaxation techniques, home practice with small thermometers & home BP monitoring.	End of treatment results: 30 of 42 medicated patients eliminated medications and maintained a reduction of 15/10mm Hg. 9 of the 42 patients cut medications by ½ and maintained a reduction of 18/10mm Hg. Only 3 of the medicated patients showed no improvement. In addition, reduction in BP achieved significance at .0001. 33 month follow-up: All patients maintained improvement.	

Abbreviations: B = Baseline; E = Experimental Group; C = Control Group; T = Treatment

In examining the work of Patel and her associates (Patel, 1973; Patel, 1975; Patel & North, 1975; Patel & Carruthers, 1977; and Patel, Marmot, & Terry, 1981) the essential ingredients for successful treatment of essential hypertension clearly emerge. These are:

(1) *Goal:* to achieve mastery of generalized and deep relaxation at the clinic and at home;

(2) *Method:* systematic feedback relaxation training i.e. autogenic training, meditation, diaphragmatic breathing, meditation (body scan) with feedback from GSR and EMG;

(3) *Extended training and transfer of training:* homework training, stress management training, and short relaxation exercises (deep breathing used with phrases such as "relax");

(4) *Coaching:* clear instructions and encouragement based on a "teacher-student" model of learning;

(5) *Mastery:* demonstration of learning in response to stressor challenges i.e. cold pressor and exercise tests.

In addition to signficant decreases in blood pressure, Patel's patients showed significant decreases in medications, serum cholesterol, triglycerides, and fatty acids (Patel & Caruthers, 1977, Patel et al., 1981).

Elements of Patel's model have been successfully replicated by other researchers. Moeller and Love (1974), and Love, Montgomery, and Moeller (1974) included four of the essential ingredients in their study: (1) the goal of generalized deep relaxation, (2) the method of systematic feedback training: autogenic training assisted with EMG feedback, (3) extended training and transfer of training: homework training, and (4) coaching: clear instructions and encouragement. An eight month follow up showed that subjects who continued to regularly practice home training further decreased pressures.

Sedlacek, Cohen, and Boxhill (1979) in a successful study included four of the five essential ingredients: (1) the goal of generalized deep relaxation, (2) the method of systematic feedback training: diaphragmatic breathing, imagery, and autogenic training assisted with EMG and thermal feedback, (3) extended training and transfer of training: home practice, and (4) coaching: clear instructions and encouragement.

Significant additions to the treatment model for essential

hypertension originated with the Menninger Foundation group (Green, Green, & Norris, 1980 and Fahrion, Norris, Green, & Green, 1986). They include four of the essential ingredients of successful training but refined and systematized the procedures, and added training to criterion on hand temperature (95+°F), EMG forehead (3 μV p-p), and most importantly, foot temperature to 92+°F. An essential element of their program is extensive feedback training at home and the completion of home training records. Subjects train on hands and feet daily and monitor blood pressure before and after each home training session. Ingredient four, coaching, includes a detailed rationale that explains how perceptions alter physiology and how feedback assisted training works. In addition they encourage patients to take responsibility for improving lifestyle. Fahrion and colleagues are currently conducting a large controlled group study of this training model, funded by the National Heart, Lung, and Blood Institute.

Blanchard and Andrasik (Blanchard et al., 1984) at the Center for Stress and Anxiety Disorders have also developed a training procedure based on the Fahrion and Green model. While Blanchard originally used direct feedback of blood pressure (Blanchard et al., 1977), his work has evolved with developments in the field. Blanchard and his associates are now applying a systematic autogenic temperature feedback training approach to the treatment of essential hypertension with successful results. An addition to the treatment model of this group is the use of simple mastery tasks: (1) asking the patient to warm hands on command with no feedback; (2) demonstrating self regulation skills in response to stressors such as a cold pressor, mental arithmetic, and stressful imagery. The results of this thermal feedback training study demonstrate a clinically and statistically significant effect for the treatment of essential hypertension (Blanchard et al., 1984).

These studies indicate that a model of systematic biofeedback training and stress management for essential hypertension is successful. Direct blood pressure feedback studies have failed with the exception of Krisst and Engel (1975). Krisst and Engel's study, however, included self control and self management training. Patel's work with a team at the National Heart, Lung, and Blood Institute (Frankel et al., 1978) included direct blood pressure feedback but removed many of the essential ingredients. The study was unsuccessful. The report states: ". . . For these patients the frustration experienced in unsuccessfully coping with the demands of the blood pressure and EMG feedback procedures may have contributed to a pressor effect . . ." (Frankel, Patel, Horwitz, Friedewald, & Gaarder, 1978, p. 287). When Patel returned to the original model that included GSR feedback, breathing exercises and stress management training, her work was again successful (Patel, et al., 1981).

Biofeedback Training for Treatment of Headache

The original impetus for treatment of headache with biofeedback training developed from the models and work of Budzynski and Stoyva (Budzynski et al., 1973, and Stoyva & Budzynski, 1974) and Green, Green, and Walters (1970). The original study by Budzynski et al., (1973) triggered a flurry of research on the use of EMG biofeedback training for the treatment of tension headache. Budzynski's research and other successful studies are summarized in Table 3.

Table 3
Successful Clinical Biofeedback Training for Migraine,
Tension, & Mixed Headache

Study	Treatment	Training Results	Symptom Result
Budzynski et al 1973, control group outcome E=6, C1=6: False feedback, C2=6: Waiting list control	T: EMG (forehead) 16 sessions—home practice (same as in lab) (goal was explained as deep relaxation) B: 2 sessions	E=10 μV to 3 μV (p-p), C1=10 μV to 6 μV (p-p). +.90 correlation between training & treatment effect. Cross-over design training for C1 & C2 if desired. (8 chose to be trained, 6 achieved a significant training & treatment effect.)	E=.001 decline in tension headaches at 30 mo. follow-up; significant decrease in meds. 18 mo. follow-up (4 located—3 maintained decrease while 1 had moderate reduction (same individual with minimal training effect.)

Table 3 continued

Study	Treatment	Training Results	Symptom Result
Hutchings & Reinking, 1976 control group outcome: E1=6, E2=6, E3=6	B: 28 days for Symptom, B: 3 sessions, T1: Relaxation tapes (15 min) (Progressive, Autogenics, Passive Volition), T2: Relaxation tapes + EMG (forehead) (30 min.), T3: EMG (forehead) (15 min.)—"keep signal as low as possible" (home practice twice a day based on what learned in laboratory)	E=20μV to 7.5μV(p-p) to 9μV (follow-up), E2=16 to 5.5μV(p-p) to 5 (follow-up), E3=19 to 6μV(p-p) to 5+ (follow-up)	E1=20% reduction in headache (15 to 11), E2=66% (14 to 3) E3=66% (10 to 3); (headache scores computed by multiplying # of headache hours times average intensity for the day)
Raskin, Johnson, & Rondestvedt (1973), group outcome, 4 muscle tension headache patients.	B: 8 weeks Train to criterion, 2.5 μV p-p (forehead) Home practice twice a day. Relaxation exercises.	All four achieved criterion averaged over 25 minute period.	All four achieved significant symptom reduction for frequency, intensity, and duration of headache using Budzynski's quantification scale.
Blanchard et al., 1982, group outcome study, 33 tension headaches, 30 migraine, 28 mixed. All were given 10 sessions of relaxation training. Those who had not achieved 60% symptom reduction were given biofeedback training.	14 migraines, thermal biofeedback, 15 tension headache, EMG biofeedback, 14 mixed headache, thermal biofeedback, all had 12 sessions of home practice and cue-controlled exercises	not reported	6 migraine; 7 tension; & 9 mixed; achieved significant (statistical & clinical) reduction in frequency and duration of headaches.

Table 3 continued

Study	Treatment	Training Results	Symptom Result
Jurish, et al., 1983; group outcome study. 40 migraineurs or combined migraine & tension	Tc: 20 clinic based (11.39 hrs. of therapist time), Th: 20 home based (2.59 hrs. of therapist time), Tc received 12 sessions of relaxation; Tc received 10 thermal biofeedback sessions in clinic; Th group received three clinical sessions (1) relaxation (60 min.), (2) temperature (60 min.) and (3) final visit (30 min.). Th group received 7 manuals & five audio-tapes. Both groups did home practice in warming hands with the use of small thermometers.	Clinic based group achieved 93°F in self-control task & 94°F in training	78% of home based group achieved 50% or greater decrease in headache index. 52.4% of clinic based group achieved 50% or greater decrease in headache index. Both groups complied equally with home training requirements. 61.5% success rate for mixed headache, 45.3% success rate for migraineurs.
Libo & Arnold, 1983b. 7 migraine, 5 tension headache, 13 mixed headache	Trained to criterion on EMG forehead (1 RMS microvolt) and 95°F. on hands with temperature feedback, 5 to 7 relaxation techniques were taught for home practice e.g. autogenics, progressive, meditation, guided imagery, etc.	All subjects reached criterion.	Follow-up between 1-5 years, 25 of 27 retained complete symptom relief, 1 tension headache person relapsed, and 1 mixed headache found a new medication.

Abbreviations: B=Baseline; E=Experimental Group; C=Control Group; T=Treatment; Tc=Treatment group at Clinic; Th=Treatment group at home.

Tension Headache

The early study of Budzynski et al., (1973) was a good beginning model for biofeedback training research: (1) adequate baselines (two 30 minute no feedback sessions and two weeks of symptom charting); (2) subjects trained to deep levels of relaxation (3 microvolts peak-peak, forehead); (3) correlating the training effect with the treatment effect (+.90); (4) lengthy follow-up (one year); (5) using a crossover design in which the control subjects receive biofeedback training. Budzynski referred to this model as a "bare-bones" procedure (1973) and in training the cross-over control subjects added relaxation cassette tapes and a portable EMG unit for home use.

Several early studies replicated Budzynski's model by training subjects to levels of deep relaxation (Raskin, 1973; Hutchings & Reinking, 1976) and achieved successful clinical results for tension headache. Unfortunately, many studies on biofeedback training for treatment of headache either did not report training data (Chesney & Shelton, 1976; Haynes et al., 1975; Fried et al., 1977; McKenzie et al., 1974), did minimal training of 1 to 3 sessions (See Table 1 in Error 1), or failed to include many of the other essential ingredients that are necessary for successful biofeedback training, as discussed in the methodological errors and in this chapter.

Recent studies have successfully replicated the model of Budzynski, Stoyva, and Peffer (1977). In a long term follow up study, Libo and Arnold (1983b) demonstrated that patients who achieved training criteria of 95°F on hands and 1 microvolt (RMS) on forehead successfully alleviated tension headaches.

In a successful study on tension headache, Blanchard et al. (1982) used systematic feedback training (EMG feedback with systematic relaxation exercises); they also included home training and clear instructions. A contribution to this training model is a demonstration of muscular relaxation in the absence of feedback (Blanchard et al., 1982).

Migraine Headache

The discovery that biofeedback training could be effective for the treatment of migraine headache led to numerous studies that used a variety of training techniques in isolation or combined: autogenic training, progressive relaxation, EMG training, temperature biofeedback training, autogenic feedback training. Double-blind studies (Kewman & Roberts, 1980) and minimal training studies (Price & Tursky, 1976) resulted in no learning and no symptom reduction.

In a meta-analysis of relaxation techniques for treatment of migraine Blanchard (1982) reported: (1) Thermal feedback relaxation with autogenic training achieved a 65.1% success rate with 146 patients; (2) Thermal feedback relaxation achieved a 51.8% success rate with 41 patients; (3) Relaxation training (progressive relaxation or the relaxation response) achieved a 52.7% success rate with 159 patients. In contrast medication placebos achieved a 16.5% success rate with 234 patients. There was no statistically significant difference between the three relaxation groups although the autogenic feedback training group showed a slight "arithmetic advantage."

A major difficulty in a meta-analysis is the absence of training data. Fahrion (1977) showed a 71% success rate at a six month follow-up after training 21 migraineurs to 95°F on hands using autogenic feedback techniques. The long term follow-up study by Libo and Arnold (1983), however, showed a 100% success rate with migraineurs who achieved training criteria of 95°F on hands *and* 1 microvolt (RMS) on forehead.

Two recent studies on migraine headache and mixed headache (Blanchard et al., 1982, and Jurish et al., 1983) demonstrated significant clinical results using autogenic feedback training with home practice, clear instructions, clear rationale and demonstration of learning tasks such as increasing hand temperature on command without feedback.

Jurish et al. (1983) compared a home based training group and a clinic based training group. Both groups were given several types of relaxation procedures and thermal feedback. It is interesting that symptom reduction in the home based group exceeded that of the clinic based training groups, 78.9% to 52.4% in spite of the fact that both groups did equal amounts of training. There is no ghost in the clinic either.

Raynaud's Disease and Biofeedback Training

Double-blind and "bare-bones" studies for treatment of Raynaud's disease have been ineffective. Biofeedback training studies that are successful in the treatment of Raynaud's disease, train patients to deep levels of relaxation and hand warming, and, to mastery during cold stressors. Freedman, Ianni, and Wenig (1983) conducted the most successful study for the treatment of Raynaud's disease. They compared four groups: (1) finger temperature feedback, (2) finger temperature feedback under cold stress, (3) autogenic training, and (4) forehead EMG. Each patient did home training and received cognitive stress management 10 minutes before and after each clinic training session. Frequency of symptom was reduced by 92.5% for the temperature biofeedback under cold stress group, 66.8% for the temperature biofeedback group, 32.6% for the autogenic training group, and 17.0% for the EMG training group. Teaching patients to master self regulation with biofeedback training in the face of cold stress was clearly the most effective. The model used by Freedman et al., is similar to the other models for the treatment of essential hypertension, migraine headache, mixed headache, and tension headache. The model includes: (1) *goal*: deep relaxation and blood flow control, (2) *method:* systematic feedback training i.e. autogenics, thermal feedback etc., (3) *extensive training and transfer of training:* home training, (4) *coaching:* clear instructions, cognitive training, and (4) *mastery:* training subjects to master cold stressors.

Biofeedback Training for other Disorders

Other areas of successful biofeedback treatment in which extensive training is done and clear instructions are provided include the following:

(1) Insomnia: Hauri, (1981); Hauri, Percy, Hellekson, Hatmann, & Russ (1982);

(2) Neuromuscular disorders: Brudny, Korein, Grynbaum,

Belandres, and Gianutsos, (1979); Finley, Niman, Standley, and Ender (1976); Hurd, Pegram, and Nepomuceno (1980); Krebs (1981); Middaugh (1978); Wolf (1980);

(3) Chronic Pain: Nouwen and Solinger (1979); Wolf et al. (1982);

(4) Attention Deficit Disorders: Carter and Russell (1983); Denkowski, Denkowski, and Omizo, (1983); Lubar and Lubar (1984);

(5) Motion Sickness: Cowings and Toscano (1982); Toscano and Cowings (1982);

(6) Epilepsy: Lubar and Bahler (1976); Sterman (1973); Sterman and MacDonald (1978); Sterman, MacDonald, and Stone (1974);

(7) Irritable Bowel Syndrome: Giles (1981); Neff and Blanchard, (1985);

(8) Subvocalization: Aarons (1971); Hardyck, Petrinovich, Ellsworth, (1967); Hardyck, and Petrinovich, (1969);

(9) Fecal incontinence: Cerulli, Nikoomanesh, and Schuster (1979); Latimer, Campbell, and Kasperski, (1984); Wald (1981);

(10) Urinary incontinence: Burgio, Robinson, and Engel, (1985); Burgio, Whitehead, and Engel, (1983); Middaugh, Whitehead, Burgio, and Engel, (1985).

(11) Generalized anxiety and panic disorders: Cohen, Barlow, Blanchard, Di Nardo, O'Brien, and Klosko (1984).

Applied Clinical Biofeedback Studies and the Mastery Model

The power and depth of biofeedback training are most clearly seen in single case clinical reports and long term follow up studies of patients treated in biofeedback clinics (see Tables 4 and 5 at end of chapter). It is in clinical practice that the mastery model is most fully developed.

The Mastery Model

Elements of the mastery model for clinical practice were first systematically described by Stoyva and Budzynski (Budzynski,

1973; Budzynski & Stoyva, 1972; Stoyva & Budzynski, 1974; Budzynski, Stoyva, & Peffer, 1977). Their criteria for successful clinical training is mastery in three domains, physiological, cognitive, and behavioral.

The details of this mastery model and its refinements as applied to psychophysiological disorders are as follows:

(1) Goals with clear criteria:

(a) Physiological mastery: This includes: (1) Cultivated, generalized low arousal—defined by Budzynski et al. (1977) as low arousal on three parameters, EMG, hand warming and EDR. These researchers defined low arousal as 2.5 microvolts peak-to-peak on forehead and forearm, 90°F hand temperature, and 2 micromohs (EDR). Since then research by Libo et al., (1983), Fahrion (1978), Green, et al, (1980), and our own work (Shellenberger et al., 1983, Shellenberger, et al., 1986) indicate that criterion should be as high as 95°F on hands and 92°F on feet; (2) and learned control of specific physiological processes such as finger tip blood flow in migraine and Raynaud's patients, blood pressure in hypertension, and EMG in tension headache.

(b) Cognitive mastery: The ability to: (1) rapidly change perceptions, (2) permanently change maladaptive perceptions, (3) identify irrational thinking, (4) dispute irrational thinking, (5) maintain cognitive flexibility, and (6) maintain cognitions of personal power and personal responsibility for health.

(c) Behavioral mastery: The ability to transfer both physiological and cognitive skills to any situation, to achieve healthy psychophysiological homeostasis and maintain homeostasis when encountering stressors, or to recover from stress rapidly.

(2) Method: systematic feedback training techniques such as breathing exercises, body scan, autogenic training, quieting response, and progressive relaxation assisted by EMG, thermal, EDR, and EEG feedback.

(3) Extended training and transfer of training: homework training and practice records, desensitization, flooding, stress management practice, and short relaxation exercises.

(4) Coaching: clear instructions and rationale, encouraging successful behaviors, positive interaction with the patient, and positive expectancies. Coaching focuses on the unique strengths and limitations of the trainee; a program is created for the individual.

(5) Mastery Tasks: demonstration of self-control without feedback in relaxed settings (i.e. increase temperature on feet to 92°F or more in 5 minutes), demonstration of self-control without feedback in stressful situations, i.e. cold room, cold pressor test, stress profile, performance tasks, and interpersonal confrontations.

A major emphasis in this model is the use of desensitization and stress management procedures for training to high levels of mastery. The early articles by Budzynski and Stoyva focus on the importance of biofeedback instrumentation for desensitization procedures and the importance of desensitization procedures for mastering the use of low arousal skills during life stressors (Budzynski & Stoyva, 1972 and Budzynski, 1973). This element of training has not been included in research studies.

The effectiveness of the mastery model is seen in the many successful cases reported by clinicians (Table 4). The case study of three stutterers reported by Craigh and Cleary (1983) is exemplary. The patients were first trained to EMG criterion of 4 microvolts (peak-peak) or less on forehead. Second, subjects were given three challenging situations: (1) read and converse fluently in the clinic in the presence of strangers, while lowering EMG feedback; (2) read and converse fluently in the clinic in the presence of strangers without feedback; (3) converse fluently in a cafeteria, without EMG feedback. Finally, maintenance techniques were taught: self reinforcement, self monitoring, and self practice.

A mastery model provides clear procedures for maximum performance training. By establishing high goals, the trainee is encouraged to achieve maximum success in psychophysiological self regulation and symptom reduction, and training will necessarily be thorough. The success of the model depends upon skilled clinicians who are good coaches and teachers, who can establish realistic goals appropriate to the individual, and can develop ingenious stressors for demonstrating mastery.

The mastery model provides guidelines for research and clinical practice that will eliminate the hit-and-miss approach of many research studies. And finally, the mastery model allows the experimenter or clinician to know with certainty that the trainee has learned, overcoming the problems of adaptation and variability. The exact parameters of the mastery tasks and criteria for psychophysiological mastery are unique to the trainee, and must be developed in relation to symptoms and life stressors.

Perhaps if prizes were given for a Biofeedback Olympics, this model for biofeedback training and the mastery of somatic and autonomic self regulation would hastily be accepted by all.

Clinical Biofeedback Practice

Biofeedback training is, above all, a clinical tool. This is because psychophysiological feedback for psychophysiological self regulation is, theoretically and practically, in the domain of health. When biofeedback training is used in clinical settings, in which it is properly understood, the maximum potential of the tool, and the maximum potential of the trainee, are demonstrated. For this reason, we include below the salient elements of clinical practice. The elements of clinical practice are in strong contrast to traditional research.

Unlike "official doctrine" research training, applied clinical biofeedback training includes:

(1) A clinician trained in individual assessment.
(2) A clinician trained to effectively interact with patients. Research studies use technicians, graduate students, or research psychologists with minimal interpersonal skills. In addition, research designs often eliminate interaction between trainer and trainee and create impersonal environments.
(3) A certified or licensed clinician. Clinicians are required to demonstrate therapeutic and biofeedback training skills. Researchers are not certified, nor do they need to demonstrate knowledge of biofeedback training and therapy.
(4) A clinician who can creatively design unique training programs for each patient. Research studies have continually failed to design unique training programs for individuals. A standard training protocol is used with all subjects.
(5) A multicomponent procedure that maximizes treatment for each individual. Official doctrine research dilutes treatment effectiveness by using simplistic training procedures and a single biofeedback component.
(6) A flexible protocol. Clinicians are able to adapt training pro-

cedures to life changes of their patients. Research studies follow a set training procedure throughout the study.
(7) Goals of stress management and enhancing the quality of life. Clinicians focus on symptom reduction, prevention, stress management and enhanced quality of life. Researchers do not focus on broad effects such as "enhanced quality of life" and are not necessarily "invested" in symptom reduction, if it is not a specific effect of the independent variable. The use of double-blind design is an example.
(8) A mastery model of biofeedback training.

There are so many major differences between experimental biofeedback training studies and clinical practice that the external validity of biofeedback research conducted in laboratories is questionable.

In conclusion, we have a clear model for successful biofeedback training. Evidence for this comes from: (1) control group studies (Tables 2, & 3, and the studies cited in "Biofeedback Training for Other Disorders;" (2) long term follow-up studies (Table 5); and (3) systematic case reports (Table 4). In examining the models for successful treatment described in these studies, we find that the protocol is essentially the same for a variety of disorders and therefore has been tested repeatedly over the years. These studies use a training protocol that, when followed, leads to clinically significant results. These results are not idiosyncratic to a few patients and clinics, but are "universal." The protocol, including systematic feedback training, results in significant and lasting treatment effects, in some cases with patients who have had symptoms for many years and have undergone a variety of other treatments as exemplified by the many studies listed in Table 4.

The most valuable information for clinicians comes from the single case reports and follow-up studies of clinicians who have creatively treated a variety of difficult patients. These reports are of equal value to researchers who are interested in determining the elements of successful training.

Elements of the mastery model have been used from the beginning of biofeedback applications, and it has evolved into a powerful multi-component approach to psychophysiological self regulation. If essential elements are removed, training is less effective; as elements are included in the treatment protocol, learning and symptom reduction are facilitated.

Many researchers and clinicians have reported successful results, and yet, the status of biofeedback training is still questioned.

In the next chapter we examine the conditions that lead to the rejection of successful biofeedback studies by researchers of the official doctrine.

Table 4
Systematic Case Studies

Subjects	Treatment	Results
Campbell & Latimer, 1980. 22 yr. old female with urinary retention.	Feedback of intravesical pressure with a urinary catheter (7 sessions). Behavior analysis and therapy were used.	After 6 months of treatment, she was symptom free. No relapse during a 9 month follow-up.
Carlsson & Gale, 1976, 59 yr. old female with TMJ for over five years.	EMG assisted relaxation training of masseter muscles.	Symptom free at 1 year follow-up.
Craigh & Cleary, 1982, 3 male stutterers, ages 10, 13 & 14.	Phase I: 3 EMG sessions 60 minutes each for relaxation mastery tasks; Phase II: EMG feedback while speaking; train to criterion of 4 μV (p-p); Phase III: transfer of training—EMG feedback while speaking in front of strangers, and speaking in front of strangers in public setting.	Reduction of stuttering and stabilization of speaking by all 3 patients.
Dietvorst & Eulberg, 1986, Treatment of a cold limb in a post-polio patient. Patient was unable to tolerate cold weather or excessive air conditioning.	Systemic biofeedback training for foot warming. Autogenics, progressive, diaphragmatic breathing, and home training with portable temperature unit. Goal was training to mastery—demonstration of foot warming. (12 sessions).	Results in training showed: Consistent increases of 5.72°F. to achieve 89°F. on foot. Demonstrated this ability 7 times. Demonstrated in last sessions the ability to increase temperature from 78.8°F. to 92.3°F. Outdoor temperature was 0°F., indoor temperature was 68°F. At 12 month follow-up patient was able to warm affected limb & shovel snow for two hours.

Table 4 continued

Subjects	Treatment	Results
Duckro, Pollard, Bray, & Scheiter, 1984, middle aged man with complex tinnitus, before biofeedback treatment he had received 6 months of psychotherapy.	Introduced to progressive relaxation then to EMG (frontal) feedback. Muscle tension was easily reduced and then had 16 temperature feedback sessions on hands.	Tinnitus was reduced from severe to mild. Severe depression was eliminated. Severe anxiety was reduced to mild. He learned to increase temp from 83°F. to 95°F.
Fritz, 1985, cluster headache patients, two chronic & four episodic. All six had a history of at least six years of cluster headache.	EEG & Open Focus training	Two yr. follow-up for 4 patients and 1 yr. follow-up for 2 patients—5 reported complete remission and 1 reported significant decreases in frequency.
Hand, Burns, & Ireland, 1979, 56 yr. old Parkinsonian female with lip hypertonicity	EMG feedback training with speech therapy (6 sessions).	At end of treatment patient achieved voluntary control of both isometric & anisometric states of contraction and relaxed muscular levels in postural states.
Hoelscher & Lichstein, 1983, Chronic Cluster Headache for over 20 years, 1-5 attacks a day, 61 yr. old male.	Blood volume pulse feedback (14 sessions), home practice each day. Baseline: 18 days.	70% reduction in frequency and 45% decrease in severity—large decreases in medications (100% decrease in narcotics, 70% decrease in antimetics, 75% decrease in migraine abortives, 2 yr. follow-up showed decreases were maintained.)
Inz & Wineburg, 1985, sympathectomized Raynaud's disease patient, female, age 45. Raynauds's for 9 yrs. and in danger of losing first digit of right hand.	6 temp & autogenic sessions with probe on first digit of right hand with no improvement, 7th session with probe on second digit of right hand, 8th & 9th sessions probe on first digit of right hand.	7th session increased temp 13.3°F. in second digit, and 8 and 9 sessions increased first digit to 85°F. or more. Patient consistently demonstrated baseline temp of 85+°F. on 8th & 9th sessions.

Table 4 continued

Subjects	Treatment	Results
King & Arena, 1984, chronic cluster headache, 69 yr. old male with 37 yr. history of headaches once a day and head pain at night.	7, 30 minute temp sessions assisted by a variety of cognitive & relaxation strategies, home practice, self monitoring, and spouse contingency program.	15 mo. follow-up showed headaches reduced to 1 a week, pain was significantly reduced and medications reduced by 100%.
Latimer, 1981, diffuse esophageal spasm, 41 yr. old female with history of symptom now considering a long esophageal myotomy.	Progressive relaxation, EMG (frontal) feedback, home practice, and feedback of esophageal motility & double swallowing technique.	6 mo. follow-up showed she could eat all foods & reduced spasm to 6 min. a week.
LeVine, 1983, 30 yr. old female, a functionally impaired professional violinist.	Thermal feedback (6 sessions) with in vivo feedback exercises practiced at home.	Four year follow-up still symptom free.
Levee, Cohen, & Rickles, 1976, Relief of tension in facial and throat muscles of a woodwind musician, alcoholic, 52 yr. old male.	EMG (forehead) relaxation feedback and psychotherapy.	End of treatment patient is symptom free with enriched family & work life.
Libo, Arnold, Woodside, Borden & Hardy, 1983, functional bladder-sphincter dyssynergia, 8 yr. old female.	14 (60 min.) sessions of EMG tense-relax training of perineal musculature, home practice of relaxation during voiding and Kegel exercises.	Symptom free, maintained at 1 year follow-up.
Marrazlo, Hickling, & Sison, 1983, 15 yr. old girl with migraine & tension headaches since age 3. Medications were not helping and she was missing three days of school per week.	Cognitive training, EMG and temp autogenic feedback, home training using imagery & autogenics.	18 mo. follow-up disclosed she was totally free of migraines & had only mild tension headaches occasionally.

Table 4 continued

Subjects	Treatment	Results
Norton, 1976, 34 yr. old female, eye closure reactions, 13 yr. history of difficulty keeping eyes open.	General relaxation training at home and in the clinic assisted with EMG forehead feedback, negative practice of exaggerating eye closures & tensing facial muscles.	6 month follow-up: normal eye closures; engagement in new social activities.
Olton & Noonberg, 1982, 21 yr. old female, migraine.	B: 74°F; B: 1 every two weeks; T: 20 Thermal sessions. Home practice of Benson's relaxation & stress management	1 yr. follow-up only 2 headaches. —Increase hand temp 5°F. in five minutes. —Base temp now 90°F.
Olton & Noonberg, 1982, 52 yr. old female, migraine headaches, extensive medications	B=84°F.; b=headaches (50 yrs.); T=18 autogenic feedback sessions home practice of muscle relaxation exercises	Eliminated medication. —achieve 95°F. in 7 min. —decrease frequency by 73%
Peck, 1977, Blepharospasm, (spasmodic winking), 50 yr. old female.	17 EMG sessions, placements on left frontalis & lower orbicularis oculi muscles.	Reduction from 1600 spasms per 20 min. to 15, massive contraction reduced to ordinary blink. 4 mo. follow-up retained improvement.
Reeves, 1976, 20 yr. old female, 5 yr. history of tension headache	Phase 1: B: $9\mu V$ (RMS); Phase 2: 6 sessions of cognitive training; Phase 3: 18 forehead EMG relaxation training.	66% decrease in headache activity maintained at 6 mo. follow-up.
Rosenbaum, 1983, insulin treated diabetes mellitus; 18 yr. male; 27 yr. female; 17 yr. female, 25 yr. female, 71 yr. male, 61 yr. female.	Budzynski's System Approach (EDR, EMG, & Temp to criterion), psychotherapy as adjunctive treatment.	4 yr. follow-up shows significant improvement.

Table 4 continued

Subjects	Treatment	Results
Shulimson, Lawrence, & Iacono, 1985, 3 males in their 50's with diabetic ulcers.	22-27 temp sessions, home practice with tapes & liquid crystal thermometer, probe in clinic placed on border of ulcer.	1st subject increased temp consistently and had complete healing of ulcer; 2nd subject increased temp consistently and had almost total healing of the ulcer; 3rd subject did not consistently increase temp and had no healing.
Tansey, Bruner, 1983, 10 yr. old hyperactive boy with developmental reading disorder.	3 EMG (frontal) sessions followed by 20 SMR sessions, relaxation instructions and rewards of toy trucks.	EMG: 60 μV (p-p) to 5 μV (p-p). Significant increases in SMR. 2 yr. follow-up: Significant improvement in reading, academic grades, ocular movement, etc.

Table 5
Follow-up Studies

Subjects	Treatment	Results
Adler & Adler, 1983, Ten year follow-up of control group outcome. E=53 migraineurs (13 classical, 34 common, 5 mixed, 1 basilar artery). 19 year previous history of headache; C=15 subjects (3 classical 12 common). 16 year history of headache.	T: Train to 95°F. on hands in relaxed & *stressed* conditions using systematic relaxation methods, home practice, psychotherapy. C: Train to 95°F. in relaxed conditions using systematic relaxation & home practice.	E=headache frequency per year decreased from 35 to 5.8; medications decreased significantly; 91% continued to practice relaxation during stressful periods. Coping with anger was the most valuable skill learned in psychotherapy. C=headache frequency per year decreased from 35 to 23; medications did not decrease significantly; 45% continued to practice during stressful periods.
Adler & Adler, 1976, 58 patients with migraine, tension, mixed & cluster headaches, follow-up from 3½ yrs. to 5	EMG, Temperature and autogenic feedback sessions, adjunctive psychotherapy.	42% had no headaches or very occasional ones, 44% reduced frequency by 75%
Ford, Strobel, Strong & Szarek, 1983, 340 patients with a variety of disorders. Follow-up varied from 3 months to 2 years.	Train to subjective criteria of relaxation using EMG, temp, quieting response training, home practice.	Raynauds=18 of 23 improved, migraines=29 of 45 improved, irritable colon=7 of 13 improved, Raynauds disease with other symptoms=9 of 15 improved, tension headache=13 of 33 improved, hypertension=5 of 15 improved, mixed headache=79 of 131 improved, others=27 of 61 improved.

Table 5 continued

Subjects	Treatment	Results
Libo & Arnold, 1983, 58 patients with follow-up of more than 6 months after treatment.	Train to criteria, 95°F. on hands, 1.1μV (RMS) on forehead EMG, home practice, relaxation & stress management	Significant improvement: migraine=100% improvement, tension=100% improvement, mixed headache=87% improvement, chronic pain=83% improvement, anxiety=100% improvement, hypertension=92% improvement.
Nakagawa-Kogan, Betrus, Beaton, Larson, Mitchell, & Wolf-Wilets, 1985, 360 patients completed training, and follow-up on 182 patients at 12 months. Comparison to a waiting list control group.	Biofeedback and Stress Management—Pre and Post Stress Profiles to assess learning.	End of treatment significance was obtained at .001 on tension headache, migraine headache, insomnia, hypertension, chronic muscle tension, and anxiety. Follow-up at 12 months: maintenance of symptom decrease at .001 confidence levels. Measures on stress profile showed a continued decrease in muscle tension and increase in blood flow to the hands compared to no-treatment control.
Rosenbaum, Greco, Sternberg, & Singleton, 1981, 93 patients=anxiety, headache, hypertension, Raynaud's phenomenon, insomnia, bruxism, tinnitus, hyperhydrosis, asthma, dysmenorrhea, others.	Budzynski systems model, systematic desensitization, progressive, autogenic, quieting response, home practice, stress management.	3-18 month follow-up: 32 very improved, 43 somewhat improved, 15 unchanged, 3 worse; 10 off med's, 21 reduced med's, 20 same med's, 7 increased med's.
Sedlacek, 1979, 20 Raynaud's patients.	EMG & Thermal feedback, autogenic and home practice, & imagery.	75% significant relief at 1 year follow-up.

Table 5 continued

Subjects	Treatment	Results
Sellick & Fitzsimmons, 1983, 48 migraineurs,	Train to criterion (1.5 microvolts RMS on forehead), bi-directional temperature change, home practice, progressive & autogenics.	75% improvement for those who met criterion, 39.3% improvement for those who did not meet criterion at 48 week follow-up.
Shellenberger, et al., 1986, No treatment control (n=79), Treatment group (n=50), Two year follow-up on no treatment control group and treatment group.	Biofeedback & Stress Management Classes, 16 EMG (forehead), 20 hand temperature, home practice, pre and post stress profiles at end of treatment.	Post assessment showed significant change (.05) compared to the control group on EMG levels & State-Trait. Symptom severity decreased at .05 on migraine headache, heart palpitations, essential hypertension, smoking, worrying, insomnia, rage, tension headache, bruxism, ulcers, low back pain, hay fever, anxiety. Stress management group significantly lowered physician visits .01 in comparison to control group.
Solback & Sargent, 1977, and Sargent, Walters, & Green, 1973, 74 patients on 5 yr. follow-up	Autogenic & thermal feedback, home practice, imagery.	55 (74%) reduced headache symptom by 74%.
Wiedel, 1985, 28 post-traumatic stress syndrome with other symptoms such as insomnia, headache, hypertension, back pain.	Train to criterion on temp, forehead EMG (2 microvolts or less p-p), coping skills training.	1 year follow-up: significant reduction in symptom severity (.01) and decrease in trait anxiety (.01) & state (.05)

Table 5 continued

Subjects	Treatment	Results
Yock, Schneider, Osterberg, & Stevenson, 1983, N=156 (105 responded to follow-up questionnaire), Treatment program for college students with a variety of disorders, migraine, tension, & mixed headache, ulcers, irritable bowel, essential hypertension, anxiety.	B: 50 minute stress profile. Treatment was EMG on forehead, temperature training on hands, relaxation techniques, home practice and stress management—mean number of sessions=7.	Six month follow-up: 77% had eliminated medications. 47% had significantly reduced or eliminated symptoms. 40% had moderately reduced their symptom(s). 10% reported slight improvement. 3% reported no improvement.—79% reported they were still practicing short relaxation skills.

5

The Tomato Effect, The Placebo Effect, and Science

> I would ask whether the focus on the disease process rather than on the patient is scientific in the best sense of the word. Have such clinical investigators and scientists not fallen into the trap called by Alfred North Whitehead "the fallacy of misplaced concreteness," which results from neglecting factors that should not be excluded from the concrete situation? Many unfortunate consequences result when an abstract idea, called a disease, is considered as if it were separated from the human being with the changes of the disease.
> Mark Lipkin, M.D.
> JAMA, July 11, 1985
> *And true of biofeedback as well.*

The Tomato Effect

The tomato effect is the rejection of an effective treatment because it does not fit an established model. Goodwin and Goodwin (1984) state: "The tomato effect in medicine occurs when an efficacious treatment for a certain disease is ignored or rejected because it does not 'make sense' in the light of accepted theories of disease mechanism and drug action" (p. 2387). Goodwin and Goodwin call this tendency in medicine the "tomato effect" because it is reminiscent of the rejection of the tomato as edible. The tomato was not eaten in America until 1820 because it did not make sense to eat something poisonous. The idea at the time was that the tomato is poisonous, being a member of the nightshade family. This belief was maintained in America in spite of the fact that Europeans had been eating tomatoes for years without harm. The evidence was in favor of the tomato, but the *belief* prevented acceptance of the evidence. The tomato effect in biofeedback training occurs when an efficacious treatment or training program is ignored, or rejected for publication, or criticized, because it does not make sense in the light of accepted theories about biofeedback training.

Many researchers have rejected the evidence from successful biofeedback studies because of mistaken *beliefs* about the nature of biofeedback training. In *The American Psychologist* and *Clinical Biofeedback and Health,* editors accepted derogatory articles on biofeedback that included the following statements: "I would like to turn now from history to the current status of clinical biofeedback research. The current status is, in a word, dismal" (Roberts, 1985, p. 940); "The snake-oil approach is one that has been adopted by many biofeedback workers" (Furedy, 1985, p. 156.).

How did a therapy shown to be effective in the treatment of many disorders become a tomato? Why are the data from successful biofeedback studies ignored, discounted and criticised? Because so many researchers and reviewers of the field believe that biofeedback is something more than feedback of information—they believe in a ghost in the box with specific effects. Researchers and reviewers who believe that biofeedback has a specific effect set up the following polarity: either biofeedback has a specific drug-like effect and follows the laws of operant conditioning or it is not effective. Therefore, any study or clinical case that is not designed to demonstrate, or does not demonstrate this nonexistent specific effect is rejected.

These beliefs about biofeedback training lead to several interrelated concepts that enhance the tomato effect: confounding variables, specific vs. nonspecific effects, the placebo effect, and scientific vs. nonscientific, all brought together in Furedy's (1985) recent article, "Specific vs. Placebo Effects in Biofeedback: Science-based vs. Snake-oil Behavioral Medicine." Based on these concepts, researchers and reviewers of the field commit "tomato errors." Tomato errors are conceptual errors based on the "ghost in the box" approach to biofeedback. Researchers are unable to accept the value of an efficacious treatment because their model of biofeedback, and of science, prevents accurate assessment of the data from successful studies.

Confounding Variables

The most common tomato error occurs when researchers insist that there must be one and only one active ingredient, one independent variable, to account for the effects of biofeedback training: physiological change or symptom reduction. Any other variable contributing to the results is a "confounding variable." The active ingredient is variously called "biofeedback," "biofeedback stimulus," "reinforcer," or "contingency" and is thought to have "specific" effects, meaning that results are causally related to the active ingredient. Confounding variables are thought to produce "nonspecific" effects and to contaminate or "confound" the results through the "placebo effect." In the official doctrine view, the presence of confounding variables is reason to reject the results of a study.

Yates (1980) defines a confounding variable as ". . . an independent variable which is *not under experimenter control* [emphasis added] and may account for significant results which are thereby incorrectly assigned to the variations in an independent variable which is under experimenter control" (p. 31). The official doctrine insists that such variables must be strenuously eliminated or controlled for in biofeedback research. And what are these confounding, nonspecific, placebo-inducing, unscientific variables that are not under experimenter control and contaminate results and mask the pure specific effect of "biofeedback?" According to researchers, they are homework, relaxation training, instructions, motivation, even the information from the biofeedback instrument.

Yates (1980) discounts the research studies of Patel and associates because: "In all these studies, the relaxation training was confounded with the provision of feedback" (p. 233). Alexander and Smith (1979) discount the research studies of Budzynski and associates and other successful studies because "the unique contribution of EMG feedback has been consistently confounded with both the inclusion of other relaxation methods during training and regular home practice of nonfeedback relaxation" (p. 124,125).

Hatch writes:

> Isolation of these nonspecific effects is critical to the establishment of a strong scientific foundation for

> biofeedback and for the acceptance of biofeedback therapy by the health professions. Effects due to adaptation, habituation, suggestibility, instructions, patient motivation, and treatment credibility all can be expected to affect response to a relaxation task, and the specific effects of biofeedback cannot be unambiguously assessed unless these potentially confounding variables are in fact held constant (Hatch et al., 1983, p.410).

Hatch confuses variables like adaptation that are not part of the training, with important variables like instructions and motivation, calling them all "confounding variables."
Furedy (1979) writes:

> Rather the evidence for informational biofeedback's efficacy has to be in the form of control conditions that show that an appreciable amount of increased control can indeed be attributed to the information supplied and not to other placebo-related effects such as motivation, self-instruction, relaxation and subject selection (Furedy, 1979, p. 206).

Here, the independent variable is information, and all other variables are "confounding." On the other hand:

> Coursey (1975) compared a group given contingent feedback with control groups given a constant tone, with or without specific instructions on how to relax . . . This put the controls at a distinct disadvantage, since the contingent feedback stimulus itself provided sufficient information to enable the trained subjects to discover the response of interest (Alexander and Smith, 1979, p. 117).

In this case, the information is a confounding variable, as suggested by Hatch in describing a hypothetical study comparing two treatment packages, one using EMG feedback and the other using progressive relaxation:

> Since *nonspecific effects* [emphasis added] of the two packages differ in many respects, there are many competing explanations for the observed differences. One possibility is that the biofeedback provided subjects with *information* [emphasis added] about their muscles that the relaxation group was denied, and this produced the differential effect (Hatch, 1982, p. 379).

Hatch and Coursey seem to believe that the signals from the machine should have power to create physiological change and account for differences between groups, independently of the information provided by the signals—there is a ghost in the box.

"Confounding variable" seems to be defined as anything that the reviewer believes might contaminate the results of a study. The inclusion of "not under the experimenters control" in the definition is particularly interesting, since in biofeedback training with humans that can include almost everything. When experimenters attempt to have everything under their control, including the feedback, they create conditions in which learning cannot occur, as in bare-bones, double-blind, and ABAB designs.

Should physiological change and symptom reduction data that result from motivation, expectation, practice, instructions, and all the other variables that are thought to be "confounding" be discounted in biofeedback research and clinical practice? And should these variables be discounted? Certainly not: *there is nothing else to study.* These variables are called "confounding," and the effects "placebo" only because the drug and operant conditioning models imply that some other variable is supposed to be creating the results, some active ingredient under the control of the experimenter. But in biofeedback training there is only one variable over which the experimenter may have absolute control and that is the feedback characteristics of the machine, which have no impact on physiology. There are relaxation techniques, breathing techniques, imagery techniques, there is hope and positive interaction with the instructor, there are unending varieties of internal learning strategies, cognitions and beliefs, there is feedback of information to hasten learning, and that is it. We call these *"compounding"* variables, not "confounding" variables.

Because "biofeedback" is nothing more than a mirror, with no specific power of its own, the successful biofeedback studies described in Chapter 4 are successful precisely because they incorporated these supposedly "confounding" variables, but are therefore tomatoes and ignored. On the other hand, the unsuccessful studies noted throughout this manuscript have failed precisely because they strenuously eliminated or controlled for these variables, hoping to find the ghost in the box. By accepting poor research, and creating tomatoes, official doctrine researchers inevitably conclude:

> There is, in my opinion, no convincing evidence even to suggest, let alone to establish, that biofeedback methods represent a reasonable therapeutic procedure for the treatment of migraine headache. Most of the published literature is not relevant for a critical evaluation of the effects of biofeedback procedures on migraine (Beatty, 1982, p. 220).

> Until recently, no study investigating the treatment of Raynaud's disease with skin temperature feedback used feedback to the exclusion of suggestion, autogenic training, or other relaxation procedures. However, Guglielmi (1979) recently conducted a group outcome study employing the double-blind design . . . This study, in combination with the results previously presented, argues strongly against biofeedback being the essential ingredient in the therapeutic effects that are often attributed to it (Surwit, 1982, p. 231).

> There is absolutely no convincing evidence that biofeedback is an essential or specific technique for the treatment of any condition (Roberts, 1985, p. 940).

Statements like these are common in the biofeedback literature. The irony is that researchers like Roberts and Hatch believe that biofeedback must have drug-like properties with specific effects, use research methodology such as the double-blind design in an attempt to demonstrate that power, fail to demonstrate that power since it is not there, and then claim that biofeedback is not effective. "The results of the present investigation clearly indicate that the best treatment for Raynaud's disease is warm weather" (Guglielmi, et al., 1982, p. 118). And to add to the confusion, these researchers claim that studies that are not attempting to demonstrate the specific ghost in the box effect of biofeedback (and thus incorporate such tools as relaxation training and instructions) or fail to use appropriate control groups to demonstrate the specific effect, are confounded, unscientific, and represent "snake-oil" approaches to biofeedback training (Furedy, 1985).

Specific vs Non-specific Effects

In drug studies the attempt to determine the specific effect of chemicals on physiology is legitimate, and this effect must be demonstrated to be independent of the "nonspecific" effects of human variables such as expectation. The terms "specific" and "nonspecific" are used appropriately in drug research. The isolation of specific and nonspecific effects is needed because pharmaceutical companies can only market chemicals that are shown to have specific physiological effects. Because the biofeedback instrument and the signals from it are not chemicals and have no power in themselves to create physiological change, it seems obvious that these elements of biofeedback training produce *nonspecific effects*, if it can be said that they produce effects at all. *And because relaxation, motivation, expectations, and beliefs do have the power to change physiology via neurochemical links between cortex, limbic system, hypothalamus and the pituitary-adrenal axis, these variables do have specific effects.* It is no wonder that there has been such confusion among researchers, and between researchers and clinicians. The official doctrine researchers have been searching on the wrong path for years while clinicians have known for years that "biofeedback" has no specific effects. *These researchers have totally reversed the correct referential meaning of "specific" and "nonspecific" in relation to biofeedback.* The accurate referent of "nonspecific effect" is whatever impact the biofeedback machine might have, and the accurate referent of "specific effect" is the effect that relaxation, expectation, instructions, and all other training variables and cognitions have on physiological change and symptom reduction.

No wonder there have been so many juicy tomatoes—so many good studies that are rejected because the reviewers thought that they failed to prove the specific effect of biofeedback by confounding it with "nonspecific effects." And no wonder it has been repeatedly shown that the biofeedback machine and signals coming from it have no specific effect, and that relaxation is just as powerful, if not more powerful, than "biofeedback."

Hopefully, this discussion will end the confusion of the specific and the nonspecific effects in biofeedback training and in the future it will be understood that the specific effects of biofeeedback training are related to the training procedures and not to the machine and signals from it.

The Placebo Effect

In drug research the placebo effect refers to the degree of physiological change or symptom reduction that results from any variable other than the chemical being studied. Because placebo control groups always show some level of symptom reduction, but are not given the active ingredient, it is assumed that symptom reduction results from the subject's beliefs and expectations about the "drug" being administered. If symptom reduction in the active ingredient group is not statistically or clinically different from symptom reduction in the placebo group, the drug is considered to be ineffective and cannot be marketed. This is the approach of official doctrine research in biofeedback.

Official doctrine researchers attempting to demonstrate the specific drug-like effects of biofeedback have a problem. They must eliminate the placebo effect, or account for it in the data so that the specific effect of biofeedback can be determined. Hours of discussion, pages of written material, and numerous studies have been devoted to this problem. There are two official doctrine solutions—either eliminate the confounding variables (expectation, motivation, relaxation) or make sure that the same confounding variables operate equally upon the experimental and control groups. The former approach leads to double-blind designs and "bare bones" studies in which subjects are given minimal information about how to proceed. The latter approach has led to a variety of bizarre control groups and conditions including false feedback. Furdey (1986) writes:

> Many clinicians believe that, in the clinical context, it is unfeasible to provide the science-based, pharmacology-type, double-blind, specific-effects oriented control for biofeedback. However, the specific-effects control can be modified in such a way that it is both practical to use, and still retains the ability to make valid evaluations of specific biofeedback effects.

Here is Furedy's suggestion for an appropriate control:

> . . . In the control condition the contingency or accuracy of the feedback does not have to be completely removed, because this will often lead to the discovery by the patient and/or the therapist that the conditon is a nonfeedback one. Rather, the contingency or accuracy of the feedback may simply be *degraded* rather than being completely removed (Furedy, 1985, p. 161).

This suggestion for an appropriate control in clinical settings, and the need for it, is the epitomy of confused thinking about biofeedback training—as if smudging over the mirror would enable us to better isolate the "specific effect" of the mirror.

Control Groups

Many excellent studies conducted by clinicians have been rejected or discounted because they failed to include appropriate controls. Researchers in every field know that to determine the effect of one variable independently of the effect of other variables, control groups must be used. To isolate the effect of an ingredient, whether in dog food, in a social environment, in a classroom or in a drug, the study must include matched control subjects who receive everything that the experimental subjects receive, except the independent variable being studied. This is not the case in biofeedback training. As we have noted repeatedly, there is no independent variable with specific effects that can be isolated and studied independently of "non-specific" effects. The independent variable in biofeedback training is self regulation—self regulation of psychophysiological processes such as blood flow in hands, self regulation of low arousal, or self regulation of the self. Consequently, the need for a control group, and the nature of the control group in biofeedback research is dramatically different from other research.

Yet, researchers, who believe that "biofeedback" has a specific effect that can be isolated, automatically assume that particular types of control groups must be used, and criticize clinicians for not doing so. Varieties of control groups have been invented for comparison to "biofeedback" such as relaxation control groups (Error number 8), and groups receiving bizarre and misnamed procedures such as "false feedback" "pseudofeedback" and now "degraded feedback."

The first question to ask is not, "What does a control group control for?" (Hatch, 1982), but, "Is a control group appropriate?" Control groups are not necessary when:

> (1) we want to know whether or not an individual has achieved a level of mastery, such as 95°F finger temperature in a cold room. Using the sports analogy, we do not need a control group to determine whether or not a runner can run the 100 yard dash in 9.6 seconds; we need only a stopwatch. We do not need a control group to determine a training effect when mastery is demonstrated.
> (2) the training goal and the treatment goal are the same, such as lowering blood pressure in direct blood pressure feedback, increasing hand temperature in Raynaud's disease, and vascular complications of diabetes, or increasing sphincter control in fecal continance training. When a Raynaud's patient can consistently increase blood flow in her hand, and can abort vasospasms, the training effect is the treatment effect. A control group is superfluous. (And, an ABAB design is totally inappropriate as discussed in Error #6.)
> (3) there is a high correlation between the training and the treatment effects, and when there is a high correlation

between minimal training and minimal treatment effects (Libo & Arnold, 1983b; Budzynski et al., 1973; Acerra et al., 1984). In this case, patients who fail to demonstrate learning and symptom reduction act as a legitimate *post-hoc* control group.

(4) a single case study design is used; here we refer to the subject as her/his own control, meaning that pretreatment data are the "control" data.

(5) long term effects of single case studies or multiple systematic case studies are reported. Many long term follow-up studies of clinicians are discounted for lack of control groups. These group studies are however, compilations of single cases, and as noted above each patient acts as her/his own control.

(6) we are not interested in determining the "specific effect" of a particular element in a complex treatment protocol. Rather, we are demonstrating the effects of a multi-component training program on the basis of pretreatment baselines and long term follow-up.

Control groups are appropriate when:

(1) comparisons of one type of treatment are made with another type of treatment. For example, comparison of biofeedback treatment to a medication control group is appropriate.

(2) the elements of a treatment protocol are compared. For example, in a successful treatment for migraine headache, both hand temperature and forehead EMG feedback may be used. If the researcher wants to determine the relative effect of each feedback modality, then a comparison of the combined treatment with an EMG control group and a temperature control group may be appropriate. Whether or not this would be useful research is another issue. In clinical practice a variety of feedback modalities are used in conjunction with a variety of training techniques, and the "usefulness" of any single technique is determined by the individual patient.

The attempt to determine the specific effect of "biofeedback" is inappropriate, and the use of control groups for this purpose is misleading. When control groups are used to determine the specific effects of biofeedback, the results usually indicate that "biofeedback" contributes little to the effects. This is because either (1) subjects in the "biofeedback" group failed to learn due to the methodologies of the official doctrine, (2) subjects in the control group did learn to relax, (3) both experimental and control groups were adequately trained, and the addition of feedback did not significantly enhance learning.

When subjects in both experimental and control groups are well trained, small differences may be expected. Certainly information is a tool for learning, and information feedback is particularly important in neuromuscular rehabilitation and fecal continence training, for example. But the information from a biofeedback machine has no power in itself, and with good training humans can learn many self regulation skills without the aid of external feedback. Particularly when generalized low arousal is the goal, humans can use their own mind/body feedback to learn.

In conclusion, the use of control groups has added little to our knowledge of biofeedback training and only confuses the field by implying that the specific effects of biofeedback can be studied independently of other variables. When this is not demonstrated on a basis of experimental vs. control group comparisons, false conclusions arise. The rejection of data from successful studies on a basis of inadequate control groups is often inaccurate.

There is No Sugar Effect

In addition to the passion to eliminate or control for the placebo effect in order to determine the specific effect of the "active ingredient" in drug research and biofeedback research, the "placebo effect" has been treated as if it were not real or genuine. The term "placebo effect" carries a negative connotation of "not legitimate" or "unscientific."

Perhaps this arises from the fact that in drug studies the placebo itself is not the real or genuine drug, but is instead sugar or saline solution; thus, the placebo effect can hardly be "real."

The "placebo effect," meaning physiological change and symptom reduction, is however, as specific and real and scientific as any effect produced by a drug. And the variables that produce these real physiological effects—motivation, expectations, hope, instructions, relaxation, imagery—are just as real as any chemical compound. (Although these variables may be more difficult to study than chemical compounds, they are no less real or "scientific.")

The term, and the concept, "placebo" should be used only in the appropriate context, drug research. The term "placebo effect," if used literally, is misnamed even in that context. This can be understood by putting it this way: "sugar" and "sugar effect." We know that sugar has no sugar effect; the physiological effects result from the belief and expectation about the "drug" being consumed. In drug research the placebo is indeed an inactive ingredient. The inaccurately termed "placebo effect," however, is a specific effect not resulting from the inactive ingredient sugar, but resulting from the "active" and powerful ingredients of positive beliefs and expectations.

Are hope and positive expectation "placebos?" Certainly not in the sense of the inactive "placebo" compound that cannot create physiological change in drug studies. Therefore, it is fallacious to claim that the effects of such variables are "placebo effects." Actually, they are "motivation effects" or "expectation effects." This is not merely a semantics problem; this is a conceptual problem that arises out of the drug model and has led to considerable confusion in biofeedback research.

If Miller had used the sports training model to understand biofeedback training, the placebo effect would not have been an important issue. In sports training the issue of placebo is not problematical because the "effect" is useful and encourages the development of the skill at the beginning of training. We find it curious that researchers using the model of operant conditioning with laboratory animals were untrue to the model regarding motivation and enthusiasm. Rats and pigeons are routinely kept at 80% *ad lib* body weight to ensure enthusiasm for learning, yet due to the fear of the placebo effect, humans are denied enthusiasm for successful learning in biofeedback training.

It is obvious, however, that enthusiasm and belief alone will not enable the athlete to run a four minute mile. Effective training *and* continued enthusiasm are needed to accomplish these goals. (Elevated enthusiasm before a meet, however, may give an athlete the leading edge, and is not a placebo effect.) This is true for biofeedback training.

Physiological change and symptom reduction that result from hope and positive expectation are impressive and motivating and are excellent examples to the patient of the powerful interaction of mind and body. Yet these effects may not be sustained because they are not the result of psychophysiological training and self regulation skills.

Biofeedback training, as the term implies, is training—training in deep relaxation, training in short relaxation techniques for maintaining homeostasis throughout the day, training in cognitive/perceptual skills, and training in behavioral skills. Ultimately physiological change and symptom reduction must result from such training in order to be sustained. Nonetheless, in biofeedback training it is important to create hope and positive beliefs, and positive rapport, knowing that these are powerful ingredients of therapy that will help the patient toward recovery. We do not refer to these ingredients as "placebos," nor do we refer to their effects as "placebo effects." In this regard referring to biofeedback training as "the ultimate placebo" (Stroebel & Glueck, 1973) is inaccurate even though it is meant to suggest that the mind is powerful and plays an important role in therapy. Effective training is needed and when provided, the "placebo effect" is irrelevant, or, is nonexistent.

We conclude that there are no "placebo effects" in biofeedback training. There are only the effects of the variables that are involved in learning: good or poor training, motivated or unmotivated students, good or poor coaching. These variables are *not confounding* variables but *compounding* variables that are essential ingredients in learning any skill.

Science

As American psychology came under pressure to be "scientific" and attempted to be as much like physics as possible, it adopted a model of "science" in which the mind is conceptualized as "un scientific." The mind is viewed as unmeasurable and unobservable and therefore cannot be "scientifically" studied in psychology. Biofeedback training is creating a problem for those who espouse this model of science because the key principle that underlies biofeedback training, the principle without which biofeedback as an aid to learning would not work, is that mind and body continually interact, and that *mental events have physiological correlates, and the reverse.* The mind must play a key role if biofeedback training is to be successful, but according to the official doctrine, the mind must be ruled out or "controlled for" if biofeedback research is to be "scientific." Throughout the history of biofeedback training, researchers and reviewers of the field have criticised their own colleagues and clinicians for being "unscientific" or not following "scientific principles." Sometimes this has been suggested in very condescending tones. For example:

> . . . It is, however, the responsibility of educational programs to teach students to think critically enough to be able to avoid the pitfall of allowing fallible clinical judgment to supplement scientifically derived conclusions. . . . What is needed most in training of biofeedback clinicians is a stronger dose of experimental science and its interpretation. . . . If we are not an applied *science* then we have little more to offer than any number of other groups that want to work with clients and "make them better." (Roberts, 1985, p. 940).

> . . . There is a powerful desire among health and health-related professionals to be able to provide treatment. It is incumbent upon the serious scientist to temper that noble desire with an equally noble appreciation for the value of hard evidence, and the need for caution and patience (Katkin, Fitzgerald and Shapiro, 1978, p. 286).

The failure to adopt a science-based approach to biofeedback technology means that behavioral medicine is unable to evaluate whether biofeedback of a particular system does or does not work . . . The more scientific a treatment is, the more efficacious it will be (Furedy, 1985 p. 156).

There is *not one* well controlled scientific study of the effectiveness of biofeedback and operant conditioning in treating a particular physiological disorder (Shapiro and Surwit, 1976, p. 113).

The term "unscientific" carries a negative connotation and if a study or clinician can be labeled "unscientific" the work can be ignored. This is one of the chief tools for enhancing the tomato effect. It is time to carefully examine the issues.

What is meant by "science" and "hard scientific evidence" and "controlled scientific studies"? Apparently "science" means adopting *models* and using *research* methodology appropriate to one area of science, such as drug research or operant conditioning with animals, and applying them to whatever is of interest to the researcher, in this case biofeedback training. This is not scientific. That concepts and methods may indeed be scientific in one domain, such as the physical sciences, does not mean that these concepts and methods are "scientific" when applied to another domain, such as the complex area of mind/body interaction. For example, the double-blind design, as used by Guglielmi et al., (1982) is not scientific in biofeedback research, and the data from such studies are neither accurate nor scientific.

The recent article by Furedy (1985) "Specific vs. Placebo Effects in Biofeedback: Science-based vs. Snake-oil Behavioral Medicine" so well illustrates the confusion about what is scientific and what is not, and what is "specific" and what is not, that we examine it in detail.

As the title of the article suggests, the essence of Furedy's argument is that any physiological change that can be attributed to a "specific" cause, such as a drug, is a "specific effect" and is scientific. And any physiological change that seems to be "nonspecific," (having an unspecific cause), is a placebo effect, and is due to "snake-oil." And we all know how unscientific snake-oil is. To illustrate this point, Furedy uses the example of death by bone-pointing in an aboriginal society. He writes ". . . It is quite possible that the bone in the hands of a witchdoctor with superb bedside, or rather graveside, manners would have been superior to even a modern gun, as a killing instrument. Moreover, this superiority would have been due solely to the placebo effects of the bone, rather than to any demonstrable specific effects" (p. 156).

The implication that death by bone-pointing is not a specific effect is rather amusing. What Furedy means, of course, is that the bone does not have anything like a bullet that has specific effects on the body, so death by bone-pointing cannot be a specific effect (and by his own logic, he would have to conclude that such a death is unscientific). Furedy fails to consider that certain beliefs about the bone are so powerful and so specific that they can have very specific effects, death. And these effects and their causes are well understood by anyone who has studied the psychophysiology of stress and illness. Again, we see the confusion between what is "specific" and what is not.

Furedy continues with another example: "Again, as in the case of the witchdoctor example, it is more than likely that in that society, and administered by a master salesman, snake oil through its placebo effects would have been more efficacious than a drug like aspirin with demonstrated specific effects" (p. 156). (Actually aspirin is a poor choice here, because according to Furedy and others who contend that there are "specific" and "nonspecific" effects, specific effects are those that can be clearly attributed to a specific mechanism, and so far the mechanisms through which aspirin has its effects are unknown.) In any case, Furedy then contends that "what renders a technology superstitious rather than science-based is when the evaluation of the treatment is solely in terms of placebo, when, that is, there is no genuine role for science in the evaluation" (p. 156). This is Furedy's personal definition of the role of science; we learn later in the article that the role of science is the application of double-blind designs, "The function of the double-blind arrangement is that it separates placebo effects from specific effects" (p. 159). So Furedy is a proponent of the superstitious, ghost in the box mythology of biofeedback training. Stating this clearly he writes:

> . . . There is no question that in the pharmacological evaluation of any drug, it is the specific rather than the

placebo effects that are of interest for the science-based technology of pharmacological medicine. The argument applies in the same way to that brand of behavioral medicine that seeks to employ biofeedback in a science-based rather than snake-oil or superstitious fashion (Furedy, 1985, p. 159).

According to Furedy, then, science-based biofeedback research means using methodologies, such as the double-blind design, in an effort to determine its specific effect. Since this is not done in successful biofeedback studies, he concludes: "The snake-oil approach is one that has been implicitly adopted by many biofeedback workers" (p. 156). Furedy's "science-based biofeedback research" is not possible because the biofeedback mirror has no specific effect, and because the double-blind design has no "scientific" place in biofeedback research. Such concepts and methods are not useful and will eventually be discarded.

Science and scientific methodology evolved from a need to understand nature and dispel dogma. Yet biofeedback researchers who claim to be "scientific" are blinded by a dogma that makes it impossible for them to look at the facts and know that their concepts and methodologies have failed. Many researchers have conducted ghost in the box research with numerous errors, failed to demonstrate the specific effect of "biofeedback" and concluded that biofeedback fails. These researchers have failed to critically examine their data and methodologies, and have failed to examine the "hard scientific evidence" that makes it clear that their concepts and methodologies are inappropriate to the study of biofeedback training. This is not scientific.

In summary, we see that the concepts and constraints of official doctrine research make it easy to reject good biofeedback studies. Clinicians have been repeatedly admonished by official doctrine researchers to think critically and to be skeptical about the efficacy of biofeedback training. We think that this is good advice and suggest that researchers do the same regarding official doctrine theories and research results.

6

From the Ghost in the Box to Successful Biofeedback Training

> Biofeedback is our reflection in the mirror. It is a tool for change, a way of developing the potential that is ours. The magic, the "spirit" is not in the machine, it is within us, within the self of self-regulation.
> "Biofeedback: Steering by a Star."
> Steven Fahrion, Ph.D., Presidential Address, Biofeedback Society of America, 1983

In the preceding chapters we have examined in detail the conceptualizations, models, research methodologies and results of the ghost in the box approaches to biofeedback training and the mastery approaches to biofeedback training. We have seen that in many instances these approaches are diametrically opposed and have no relationship to each other, in spite of the common use of the term "biofeedback." How did this split occur? Why were the appropriate conceptualizations of the biofeedback instrument as a mirror, and biofeedback training as a process of learning a complex self regulation skill, not adopted and used as a research model?

In our review of both theoretical papers and research reports we find that the chief proponents of the official doctrine were trained in the operant conditioning models and methodologies. Some of these researchers began their careers working with laboratory animals, and none were originally clinicians. This initial training undoubtedly provided a familiar framework for understanding the new phenomena of biofeedback training. The comfort of familiar models is known to us all. The danger of committing category mistakes, however, is directly related to our committment to familiar models.

The work of Miller and DiCara (1971) showing that curarized

rats could be operantly conditioned to change a variety of autonomic nervous system functions automatically led to the use of a similar model with humans. Furthermore, the belief that the only rigorous scientific methodology is the isolation of the effects of the "independent variable" led to the belief that biofeedback must have demonstrable specific effects. So passionate is this belief that Hatch (1982) claimed that in biofeedback research we are "uniquely blessed" because there is an independent variable, the contingency, that can be isolated and studied. And perhaps many experimental psychologists were attracted to biofeedback because the use of instrumentation provided an opportunity to collect "hard data" on a new and interesting process. The attractiveness and concreteness of the data may also have shielded these researchers from taboo, "mentalistic," concepts and from confronting the subject of mind and its interaction with body. But for whatever reason, official doctrine researchers retreat to their models for research methodology even when they have glimpses of more appropriate conceptualizations and more important issues in biofeedback training than isolating specific effects and controlling for the "placebo effect."

The work of Neal Miller is an example. In the same article in which Miller (1976) uses the analogy of removing a blindfold from a basketball player to describe biofeedback, he relies on his familiar models to discuss appropriate research. Contradicting his own analogy, he warns researchers to beware of the enthusiasm of both the doctor and the patient and writes: "Thus, a stable baseline before training begins cannot be used to rule out the placebo effect unless both the experimenter and the patients are unaware of when the training begins" (Miller, 1976). Instead of exploring a sports training model, Miller replaces the blindfolds. His concern with the placebo effect replaces his concern for learning through feedback of information.

Official doctrine researchers adopted the well established and extremely simple conceptualizations of drug and animal research. Along with the concepts from drug and animal research came the *language*, the *methods* and most importantly, the *goals* of these fields. The early focus on voluntary self regulation and human potential for self mastery was disregarded in much of the research. Instead, the inherently minimal goals of animal and drug research were accepted for humans in "bare bones" biofeedback training. The tacit acceptance of such goals enabled the errors described in Chapter 2 to persist in biofeedback research.

In contrast, to understand the new process called "biofeedback," several pioneers knew that conceptualizations for understanding this process should be based on those areas of human experience in which high levels of performance had already been demonstrated, such as the Science of Yoga. Adept yogis have demonstrated unusual levels of self mastery. It was of interest then to study the skills of yogis and to attempt to understand the conceptualizations of Yoga. Several early pioneers of biofeedback training studied unusual people and traveled to India in search of yogis who could demonstrate their powers and in search of conceptualizations with which to understand and develop biofeedback training, (Elmer and Alyce Green, Erik Peper and Gay Luce, and Barbara Brown).

These investigations expanded our horizons and supported the growing awareness that humans have extraordinary potential for voluntary psychophysiological self regulation and health. It was clear that biofeedback training could be a *method* for the investigation of this potential and a *tool* for the enhancement of this potential for health. Concepts appropriate to voluntary self regulation were discussed early in the development of biofeedback training by these researchers: "consciousness," "self awareness," "motivation," and "volition." In *Beyond Biofeedback* the Greens (1977) devote an entire chaper to the concept of volition and discuss at length the model of biofeedback as consciousness training. Such concepts are familiar to many researchers and clinicians who use the expression "voluntary self regulation" literally, and who are involved in the exploration and development of the processes of psychophysiological self regulation.

These contradictory approaches to biofeedback training give strikingly different meanings to the term "biofeedback training." As we have described in this monograph, one use of the term refers to bare-bones, trial-and-error, unsystematic biofeedback and the other refers to systematic biofeedback training, meaning that in conjunction with feedback, a systematic training procedure is used such as "autogenic feedback training." These distinctly different meanings have led to confusion and conflict. For example, when a clinician uses the term "biofeedback training" in a single case report, this refers to systematic feedback training. But the editors and reviewers of the report may have the bare-bones concept in mind and believe that this is the only appropriate methodology with which biofeedback can be studied. Consequently the report will be rejected for publication, being called "anecdotal" or "confounded" or "not a significant contribution to the literature."

The term "psychophysiological feedback training" more accurately describes the process that is called "biofeedback training" by taking into account the impact of mind on body, and recognizing that the biofeedback instrument reflects the physiological change that results from changes in both physiologial and psychological processes. The Menninger Foundation team refers to their work as psychophysiological therapy, not biofeedback therapy. In fact, because "biofeedback therapy" includes cognitive, behavioral and physiological training to achieve the goal of self regulation or mastery, in all domains, a more inclusive term is "self regulation therapy." The use of biofeedback instrumentation is one element in self regulation therapy.

A misleading implication of the term "biofeedback training" is that the use of biofeedback equipment is the training. This is like saying "stop-watch training." Athletic training is not labeled in this way because although the stop watch is useful, or even essential, in providing information, it is not a training technique in itself. In the same way, although the biofeedback instrument is useful, and perhaps at times essential, because it provides information, it is not a training technique. Thus the term "biofeedback training" is misleading and the correct term to describe the process is "self regulation training assisted by biofeedback instrumentation." Pole vault training, however, is an accurate description of that process because the pole is essential for the activity.

The term "biofeedback training" is useful only when it means *training*, with the aid of biofeedback instrumentation. Because the terms "biofeedback," "biofeedback training," and "biofeedback therapy" are part of our common language, however, we will continue to use these terms to describe our work. We propose that in the future, the process being used should be referred to as *"unsystematic biofeedback training"* or *"systematic biofeedback train-*

ing.'' Unsystematic biofeedback training will describe the barebones or trial-and-error training procedures of the operant conditioning-drug effects model, and systematic biofeedback training, or biofeedback therapy, will refer to the use of the mastery model.

We have seen that, in essence, the drug and operant conditioning models of the official doctrine do not view biofeedback training as a tool for learned self regulation, and do not facilitate learned self regulation through the research methodologies of the models. These research methodologies attempt to study biofeedback in isolation. On the other hand, the mastery model, in essence, is a learning model, and promotes learning in psychophysiological, cognitive, and behavioral domains. This model includes the use of many training techniques, and biofeedback instrumentation as a tool for learning.

Are the machines necessary? Sometimes, but not always. A biofeedback instrument is not essential for learning relaxation and for experiencing the benefits of relaxation skills, such as symptom and medication reduction. Relaxation is powerful, and if successfully learned and practiced, healthy homeostasis is enhanced. The fact that the basic elements of the mastery model are used in the treatment of a variety of disorders is evidence of the ability of mind and body to return to healthy homeostasis.

But knowledge is power, and while there is no ghost in the machine, the feedback of information from the biofeedback instrument is of value to most trainees and is essential for some. The feedback of psychophysiological information is an ingredient in self regulation training that hastens learning by removing blindfolds and by confirming self regulation strategies. In some cases, the information is so helpful that the trainee appears to be an instant learner. Ultimately, because there is no ghost in the box, the trainee dispenses with the use of the biofeedback instrument. This happens when the trainee has learned to identify and voluntarily create the desired psychophysiological response that the machine reflects. This is the goal of self regulation therapy.

Self Regulation Training

A research and clinical model appropriate to the exploration and development of human potential for self regulation must be derived from conceptualizations and models of learning that allow exploration of all possible avenues for maximizing change. Unlike the self-limiting concepts and models that led to Category Mistakes #1 and #2, the mastery model, in which training to mastery is maximized and demonstrated, is nonlimiting. As described in detail in Chapter 4, this training model incorporates appropriate instructions by an experienced trainer, progressive, and well defined goals, consistent long-term practice, adjunctive skills training, positive self talk, positive imagery, feedback enhanced consciousness, motivation and drive (volition), and a healthy lifestyle.

If the mastery model is adopted, research issues and methodology will dramatically change:

(1) The assumptions of reductionism and parsimony would not be scientifically useful—instead of stripping away the synergy of powerful multicomponent training methods and developing artificial "bare-bones" treatment, studies would be designed to maximize mastery.

(2) Simplistic models of learning based on laboratory animal research would be replaced with models of human learning. More appropriate models are Hyland's concept of person variables (1985), McClelland's theory and research on human motivation (1984), and the work of Lazarus (1975) and Meichenbaum (1976).

(3) Mastery criteria would be established for different diseases and patient variables such as age, medication use, and health habits. An important task would be to develop laboratory stressors that are effective for testing self regulation skills and for transferring these skills to the every day stressors of frustration, performance anxiety, interpersonal conflict, and life change.

(4) Training would continue to mastery.

(5) Training data would be reported and these data would be correlated with treatment effects.

(6) The function of control groups would be to compare efficacious treatments, for example, comparing a phar-

macological group to a clinical biofeedback treatment group. In addition, single case studies and group outcome studies would be valid without "official doctrine" controls because each patient acts as his/her own control.

(7) Treatment outcome variables would include reduction in the presenting symptom, reduction in secondary symptoms, medication reduction, improved quality of life and cost effectiveness.

(8) Individual differences in physiology, training needs and learning styles would be emphasized. A research and statistical model incorporating individual differences would be developed such as that recommended by Banderia et al., (1982), and Perez and Brown, (1985). A time series design methodology would be used to accurately assess individual change scores over time.

(9) New relaxation techniques would be created.

(10) Methods for motivating subjects and ensuring compliance with the training protocol would be developed.

(11) Personal learning strategies and subjective reports would be elicited as an aid to training and research.

(12) Creativity and funding would be devoted to the development of new technology for monitoring physiological processes that are still "blindfolded" such as ocular pressure, blood sugar and kidney function.

(13) The neurophysiology of stress, relaxation, hope and expectation would be studied.

We have no illusions about the difficulty of researching a process as complex as psychophysiological self regulation. The difficulty lies in the complexity of mind/body interaction, and in changing entrenched models and methodologies. Yet there are exciting horizons to explore in our ability to self regulate mind and body for health.

We anticipate that the errors that arose from inadequate conceptualizations and models of biofeedback training can be put aside, and that appropriate models and methodologies as described in this monograph can be developed, and will expand the horizons of self regulation training and treatment.

Conclusion

The advent of biofeedback instrumentation is truly momentous. Psychophysiological information previously unavailable to consciousness is made available for the first time in human history. Systematic biofeedback training, or biofeedback therapy as we often refer to the process, is unique. Unlike drugs and other manipulations, the therapeutic goal is *masterful self regulation* and the *modus operandi* is *learning,* facilitated by the feedback of information.

Although feedback of information is essential for learning, the information itself, and the instrument providing the information, have no inherent power to create psychophysiological change in humans. Research based on the belief of inherent power (Category Mistake #1) often fails because the assumption is false and methodological errors based on the false assumptions (i.e. minimal training) limit learning and self regulation. The power of the process, systematic biofeedback training, is determined solely by the user. If the user is assumed to have the learning characteristics of laboratory animals (Category Mistake #2) then biofeedback research based on this assumption often fails because the assumption is false and methodological errors based on this false assumption (i.e. no homework) limit learning and self regulation.

We propose that after 17 years of research, it is time to ask: "How can we *maximize* our potential for self regulation, symptom reduction, and enhanced quality of life through systematic biofeedback training?"

As we address this question, the conceptualizations about human learning that must inevitably evolve will be complex, and the elucidation of the dynamics of psychophysiological self regulation will be difficult. The challenge will be to discard simplistic models and simplistic "scientific" research methodology. If we must attempt to isolate the mechanisms of this process through research, let us at least avoid methodology that kills the process that we are attempting to study—so that it will not be metaphorically said of our science, "the operation was a success but the patient died."

We look forward to renewed excitement and energy in the field of biofeedback training, as researchers and clinicians work together from a strong foundation of shared conceptualizations and models, and a shared interest in exploring the dimensions of conscious self regulation in humans.

About the Authors

Judith Alyce Green, Ph.D.

Judith Green received her B. A. in Psychology from the University of Chicago and her M. A. from the Institute of Child Behavior and Development, the University of Iowa. She spent two years on research projects at Harvard University and Boston University School of Medicine before joining the Voluntary Controls Program, The Menninger Foundation, Topeka, Kansas.

Dr. Green worked for eight years at The Foundation as a researcher in clincial biofeedback training, director of biofeedback seminars, and biofeedback therapist. She conducted her doctoral dissertation research at The Foundation on brainwave feedback training for seizure reduction in epilepsy. She received her doctorate in 1976 from The Union Graduate School, Columbus, Ohio.

Judith is known for her work with the Voluntary Controls Program team, headed by her parents, Elmer and Alyce Green, that pioneered in the clinical use of biofeedback training. She has given numerous workshops throughout the country on the principles and applications of biofeedback training with adults and children. Dr. Green has published several articles on biofeedback applications, and is co-author of the popular film "Biofeedback: The Yoga of the West'' that features explorations in self regulation at The Menninger Foundation and in India.

In 1979, Judith began private practice biofeedback therapy at the Biofeedback and Stress Management Group in Boulder, and Biofeedback and Psychotherapy Associates in Greeley, Colorado. In 1983, she left the Boulder group to become an instructor in biofeedback training at the Aims Biofeedback Institute, Aims Community College in Greeley. Judith is currently in private practice in Greeley, and is the Director of the clinical biofeedback training for the clinical internship program of the Aims Biofeedback Institute.

Robert Shellenberger, Ph.D.

Robert Shellenberger is a licensed psychologist and certified biofeedback therapist. He received his doctorate from Northwestern University in 1969. Bob was a pioneer in the development of biofeedback training in an educational setting, promoting the establishment of courses and a biofeedback laboratory at Aims Biofeedback Institute, Aims Community College in 1975. Today the Biofeedback Learning Center includes ten training rooms, one group training room, two stress profiling rooms, over 150 biofeedback instruments, and five microcomputers. Bob was also instrumental in the creation of a state certified internship training program for biofeedback clinicians. Bob teaches courses on biofeedback and psychotherapy and supervises interns in this program.

Bob has conducted many workshops on biofeedback training, stress management, and personality styles, and created the workshop "Biofeedback and Psychotherapy" for the Biofeedback Society of America continuing education program.

In 1982, Bob received a grant from the Colorado Commission on Higher Education to conduct research on the reliability and validity of stress profiling at the Aims Biofeedback Institute.

Dr. Shellenberger is the Director of a private clinic, Biofeedback and Psychotherapy Associates, in Greeley. His work in biofeedback training combines teaching, therapy, and writing. Bob brings to this work a unique background in clinical psychology, phenomenology, and philosophy.

References

Aarons, L. (1971). Subvocalization: Aural and EMG feedback in reading. *Perceptual Motor Skills, 33,* 271-306.

Acerra, M., Andrasik, F., & Blanchard, E. (1984). A preliminary examination of thermal biofeedback process data from essential hypertension patients. *Biofeedback Society of America Proceedings,* 4-7, Albuquerque, New Mexico.

Achterberg, J., McGraw, P., & Lawlis, G.F. (1981). Rheumatoid arthritis: A study of relaxation and temperature biofeedback training as an adjunctive therapy. *Biofeedback and Self-Regulation, 6,* 207-223.

Adler, C., & Adler, S. (1983). Physiologic feedback and psychotherapeutic intervention for migraine: A 10-Year follow-up. In V. Pfafenrath, P. Lundberg, & O. Sjaastad (Eds.) *Updating in Headache: Proceedings of the 1st International Headache Congress,* 217-223. New York: Sringer-Verlag Press.

Adler, C., & Adler, S. (1976). Biofeedback-psychotherapy for treatment of headaches: A five-year follow-up. *Headache, 16,* 189-191.

Alexander, A. (1975). An experimental test of assumptions relating to the use of electromyographic biofeedback as a general relaxation technique. *Psychophysiology,* 12, 656-662.

Alexander, A., & Smith, D. (1979). Clinical applications of emg biofeedback, In R. Gatchel & K. Price (Ed.), *Clinical Applications of Biofeedback: Appraisal & Status,* 112-133. New York: Pergamon Press.

Allen, J. K., Blanchard, E. B. (1980). Biofeedback-based stress management training with a population of business managers. *Biofeedback and Self-Regulation,* 5, 427-438.

American Psychological Association. Standards for Educational and Psychological Tests. Frederick B. Davis, Chair. Washington, D.C.: American Psychological Association, 1974.

Ancoli, S. & Kamiya, J. (1978). Methodological issues in alpha biofeedback training. *Biofeedback and Self-Regulation,* 3, 159-183.

Andrasik, F., Blanchard, E., Neff, E., & Rodichok, L. (1984). Biofeedback and relaxation training for chronic headache: A controlled comparison of booster treatments and regular contacts for long-term maintenance. *Consulting and Clinical Psychology,* 52, 609-615.

Arena, J., Blanchard, E., Andrasik, F., Cotch, P. & Myers, P. (1983). Reliability of psychophysiological assessment. *Behavior Research and Therapy,* 21, 447-460.

Aspy, D. N. (1969). The effect of teacher-offered conditions of empathy, congruence, and positive regard upon student achievement. *Florida Journal of Educational Research,* 11, 39-48.

Banderia, M., Bouchard, M., & Granger, L., (1982). Voluntary Control of Autonomic Responses: A Case for a Dialogue Between Individual and Group Experimental Methodologies. *Biofeedback and Self-Regulation,* 7, 317-329.

Barnes, J., Bowman, E., & Cullen, J. (1984). Biofeedback as an adjunct to psychotherapy in the treatment of vaginismus. *Biofeedback and Self-Regulation,* 9 . 281-290.

Beatty, J. (1972). Similar effects of feedback signals and instructional information on EEG activity, In D. Shapiro (Ed.), *Biofeedback and Self-Control,* 253-261, Chicago: Aldine Publishing.

Beatty, J. (1982). Biofeedback in the treatment of migraine: Simple relaxation or specific effects. *Clinical biofeedback: Efficacy and mechanisms,* 211-219. New York: Guildford Press.

Bell, J. (1979). The use of EEG theta biofeedback in the treatment of a patient with sleep-onset insomnia. *Biofeedback and Self-Regulation,* 4, 229-236.

Bell, I., & Schwartz, G. (1975). Voluntary control and reactivity of human heart rate. *Psychophysiology,* 12, 339-348.

Bergman, J., & Johnson, H. (1971). The effects of instructional set and autonomic perception on cardiac control. In J. Kamiya (Ed.), *Biofeedback and Self-Control,* 262-272. Chicago: Aldine-Atherton Press.

Blanchard, E. (1979). Biofeedback and the modification of cardiovascular dysfunctions. In R. Gatchel & K. Price (Eds.), *Clinical Applications of Biofeedback: Appraisal & Status,* 28-51. New York: Pergamon Press.

Blanchard, E. (1982). Comments on the chapters by Beatty and by Surwit. In White & Tursky (Eds.), *Clinical Biofeedback: Efficacy and Mechanisms,* 232-238. New York: Guildord Press.

Blanchard, E., Andrasik, F., & Silver, B. (1980). Biofeedback and relaxation in the treatment of tension headaches: A reply to Belar. *Journal of Behavioral Medicine,* 3, 227-231.

Blanchard, E., Andrasik, F., Neff, D., Arena, J., Ahles, T., Jurish, S., Pallmayer, T., Saunders, N., Teders, S., Barron, K., & Rodichok, L. (1982). Biofeedback and relaxation training with 3 kinds of headache: Treatment effects and their prediction. *Journal of Consulting & Clinical Psychology,* 50, 562-575. (a)

Blanchard, E., Andrasik, F., Neff, D., Teders, S., Pallmeyer, T., Arena, J., Jurish, S., Saunders, N., & Ahles, T. (1982). Sequential comparisons of relaxation training and biofedack in the treatment of three kinds of chronic headache or, the machines may be necessary some of the time. *Behaviour Research and Therapy,* 20, 469-481.(b)

Blanchard, E.B., Haynes, M.R., Kallman, M.D., & Harkey, L. (1976). A comparison of direct blood pressure feedback and electromyographic feedback on the blood pressure of normotensives. *Biofeedback and Self-Regulation,* 1, 445-451.

Blanchard, E.B., & Epstein, L.H. (1978). *A Biofeedback Primer.* Reading, Massachusetts: Addison-Wesley.

Blanchard, E., McCoy, G., Andrasik, F., Acerra, M., Pallmeyer, T., Gerardi, R., Halpern, M., & Musso, A. (1984). Preliminary results from a controlled evaluation of thermal biofeedback as a treatment for essential hypertension. *Biofeedback & Self-Regulation,* 9, 471-495.

Blanchard, E., McCoy, G., Acera, M., & Gerardi, R. (1985). A sequential comparison of thermal biofeedback training and relaxation training in the treatment of moderate essential hypertension. *Biofeedback Society of America Proceedings,* New Orleans, Louisiana.

Blanchard, E., & Young, L. (1974). Clinical applications of biofeedback training: A review of evidence. *Archives of General Psychiatry,* 30, 573-389.

Borgeat, F., Hade, B., Larouche, L. M., & Bedwani, C. N. (1980). Effect of therapist's active presence on EMG biofeedback training of headache patients. *Biofeedback and Self-Regulation,* 5, 275-282.

Borkovec, T. (1982). Insomnia. *Consulting and Clinical Psychology,* 50, 841-857.

Bouchard, M., and Granger, L. (1978). The role of instructions versus instructions plus feedback in voluntary heart rate slowing. In J. Stoyva (Ed.), *Biofeedback and Self-Control,* 312-319. New York: Aldine Press.

Brawley, L., & Roberts, G. (1984). Attributions in sport: Research foundations, characteristics, and limitations. In J. Silva III & R. Weinberg (Eds.), *Psychological Foundations of Sport,* 197-213. Champaign, Ill: Human Kinetics Publishing.

Brudny, J., Korein, J., Grynbaum, B., Belandres, P., & Gianutsos, J. (1979). Helping hemiparetics to help themselves. *JAMA,* 241, 814-820.

Budzynski, T. (1973). Biofeedback procedures in the clinic. *Seminars in Psychiatry,* 4, 537-547. (a)

Budzynski, T. (1973). Somatic Optimization: Some new concepts in biofeedback. Unpublished Manuscript (Available from Biofeedback Systems, 2736 47th Street, Boulder, Colorado 80301). (b)

Budzynski, T. (1978). Biofeedback in the treatment of muscle-contraction headache. *Biofeedback and Self-Regulation,* 3, 409-434.

Budzynski, T. (1977). Systematic desensitization. Dual Cassette Tape, Catalogue No. T-35, New York: BioMonitoring Applications.

Budzynski, T. (1979). Strategies in headache treatment. In J. Basmajian (Ed.), *Biofeedback—Principles and Practice for Clinicians,* 132-151. Baltimore, Md: Williams & Wilkins Company.

Budzynski, T., & Stoyva, J. (1972). Biofeedback techniques in behavior therapy. In D. Shapiro (Ed.), *Biofeedback and Self-Control,* 437-457. Chicago: Aldine Publishing.

Budzynski, T. H., Stoyva, J.M., Adler, C.S., & Jullaney, D.,J (1973). EMG biofeedback and tension headache: A controlled outcome study. *Psychosomatic Medicine,* 35, 484-496.

Budzynski, T., Stoyva, J., & Peffer, K. (1977). Biofeedback techniques in psychosomatic disorders. In E. Foa, & A. Goldstein (Eds.), *Handbook of Behavioral Interventions,* New York: Wiley and Sons.

Burgio, K., Robinson, J., & Engel, B. (1985). Physiotherapy for stress urinary incontinence: Comparison of bladder-sphincter biofeedback and Kegel exercise training. *Biofeedback Society of America Proceedings,* New Orleans, Louisiana.

Burgio, K., Whitehead, W., & Engel, B. (1983). Behavioral treatment of stress urinary incontinence in elderly women. *Biofeedback Society of America Proceedings,* Denver, Colorado.

Campbell, D., & Latimer, P. (1980). Biofeedback in the treatment of urinary retention. *Behavior Therapy & Experimental Psychiatry.* 11, 27-30.

Carkhuff, R. & Berenson, B. (1976). *Teaching As Treatment,* Amherst, Mass: Human Resource Development.

Carlsson, S.G., & Gale, E.N. (1977). Biofeedback in the treatment of long-term TMJ pain. *Biofeedback and Self-Regulation,* 2, 161-171.

Carlson, John (1978). Biofeedback as a research tool. *Biofeedback Society of America Task Force Report,* Denver, Colorado.

Carter, J. & Russell, H. (1984). Results of a long-term federally funded program on biofeedback and learning disabilities. In J. Lubar (Ed.), *The use of EEG for diagnosis and treatment of minimal brain dysfunction syndrome and attention deficit disorders in children.* Symposium presented at Biofeedback Society of America, Albuquerque, New Mexico.

Cerulli, M., Nikoomanesh, P., & Schuster, M. (1979). Progress in biofeedback conditioning for fecal incontinence. *Gastroenterology,* 76, 742-749.

Chesney, M., & Shelton, J. (1976). A comparison of muscle relaxation and electromyogram biofeedback treatments for muscle contraction headache. *Journal of Behavior Therapy and Experimental Psychiatry,* 7, 221-225.

Cleaves, C. (1970). The control of muscle tension through psychophysiological information feedback. Unpublished doctoral dissertation, George Washington University.

Cohen, A., Barlow, D., Blanchard, E., Di Nardo, P., O'Brien, & Klosko, J. (1984). Combined EMG biofeedback and cognitive-behavioral treatment for generalized anxiety disorder and panic disorder. *Biofeedback Society of America Proceedings,* 54-56, Albuquerque, New Mexico.

Cohen, H.D., Graham, C., Fotopoulos, S.S., & Cook, M. (1978). A double-blind methodology for biofeedback research. In J. Stoyva (Ed.), *Biofeedback and Self-Control,* 306-311. New York: Aldine Press.

Cohen, J. J., (1985). Stress and the human immune response. *Journal of Burn Care and Rehabilitation,* 6,167-173.

Coursey, R. D. (1975). Electromyograph feedback as a relaxation technique. *Journal of Consulting and Clinical Psychology,* 43, 825-834.

Cowings, P., & Toscano, W. (1982). The relationship of motion sickness susceptibility to learned autonomic control for symptom suppression. *Aviation, Space, and Environmental Medicine,* June, 570 - 575.

Cox, Richard (1985). *Sport Psychology.* Dubuque, Iowa: Brown Publishing Co.

Cox, D., Freundlich, A., & Meyer, R.G., (1975). Differential effectiveness of electromyograph feedback, verbal relaxation instructions, and medication placebo with tension headaches. *Journal of Consulting and Clinical Psychology,*

43, 892-898.

Craig, A. & Cleary, P. (1982). Reduction of stuttering by young male stutterers using EMG feedback. *Biofeedbck and Self-Regulation, 7,* 241-254.

Crider, Shapiro, & Tursky (1971). Reinforcement of spontaneous electrodermal activity. In J. Kamiya (Ed.), *Biofeedback and Self-Control.* Chicago: Aldine Press.

Cuthbert, B. (1976). Voluntary slowing of heart rate: A comparison of various techniques. Unpublished doctoral dissertation, University of Wisconsin.

Dahlstrom, L., Carlsson, S. G., Gale, E.N., & Jansson, T.G. (1984). Clinical and electromyographic effects of biofeedback training in mandibular dysfunction. *Biofeedback and Self-Regulation, 9,* 37-48.

Davis, P. (1980). Electromyograph biofeedback: Generalization and the relative effects of feedback, instructions, and adaptation. *Psychophysiology, 6,* 604-611.

DeGood, D. & Adams, A.S. Jr., (1976). Control of cardiac response under aversive stimulation. *Biofeedback and Self-Regulation, 1,* 373-385.

DeGood, D., & Chisholm, R. (1978). Multiple response comparison of parietal EEG and frontalis EMG biofeedback. In J. Stoyva (Ed.), *Biofeedback and Self-Control,* 142-149. New York: Aldine Publishing.

Denkowski, K., Denkowski, G., & Omizo, M. (1983). The effects of EMG-Assisted relaxation straining on the academic performance, locus of control, and self-esteem of hyperactive boys. *Biofeedback and Self-Regulation, 8,* 363-376.

Diamond, S., Medina, J., Diamond-Falk, J., & Deveno, T. (1979). The value of biofeedback in the treatment of chronic headache: A five-year retrospective study. *Headache, 19,* 90-96.

Dietvorst, T., & Eulberg, M. (1986). Biofeedback treatment of cold limb. Submitted for publication.

Duckro, P., Pollard, C., Bray, H., & Scheiter, L. (1984). Comprehensive behavioral management of complex tinnitus: A case illustration. *Biofeedback and Self-Regulation, 9,* 459-470.

Elder, S.T., & Eustis, N. (1975). Instrumental blood pressure conditioning in out-patient hypertensives. *Behaviour Research and Therapy,* 13, 185-188.

Elfner, L., May, J., Moore, J., & Mendelson, J. (1981). Effects of EMG and thermal feedback training on tinnitus: A case study. *Biofeedback and Self-Regulation,* 6, 517-522.

Engel, B., (1972). Operant conditioning of cardiac function: A status report, *Psychophysiology,* 9, 161-177.

Engel, B., (1979). Behavioral applications in the treatment of patients with cardiovascular disorders. In J. Basmajian, (Ed.), *Biofeedback,* Baltimore, Maryland: Williams & Wilkins, 170-179.

Engel, B. and Hansen, S. (1971). Operant conditioning of heart rate slowing. In J. Kamiya (Ed.), *Biofeedback and Self-Control,* 36-47. Chicago: Aldine Publishing.

Erbeck, J.R., Elfner, L.F., & Driggs, D.F. (1983). Reduction of blood pressure by indirect biofeedback. *Biofeedback and Self-Regulation,* 8, 63-72.

Fahrion, S. (1978). Autogenic biofeedback treatment for migraine. In M. E. Granger, (Ed.), *Research and clinical studies in headache,* 47-71. New York: S. Kanger.

Fahrion, S. (1983). Guiding your course by a star. Presidential Address at Biofeedback Society of America Conference, Denver, Colorado.

Fahrion, S., Norris, P., Green, A., & Green, E. (1986). Biobehavioral treatment of essential hypertension: A group outcome study. Manuscript submitted for publication.

Fey, S., & Lindholm, E. (1976). Systolic blood pressure and heart rate changes during three sessions involving biofeedback or no feedback. *Psychophysiology,* 12, 513-519.

Finley, W., Niman, C., Standley, J., & Ender, P. (1976). Frontal EMG-biofeedback training of athetoid cerebral palsy patients: A report of six cases. *Biofeedback & Self-Regulation,* 1, 196-1982.

Ford, M., Stroebel, C., Strong, P., & Szarek, B. (1983). Quieting response training: Long-term evaluation of a clinical biofeedback practice. *Biofeedback and Self-Regulation,* 8, 265-278.

Frankel, B., Patel, D., Horwitz, D., Friedewald, W., & Gaarder, K. (1978). Treatment of hypertension with biofeedback and relaxation techniques. *Psychosomatic Medicine,* 40, 276-292.

Frankel, F. (1976). *Hypnosis.* New York: Plenum.

Freedman, R., Lynn, S., Ianni, P., & Hale, P. (1981). Biofeedback treatment of Raynaud's disease and phenomenon, *Biofeedback and Self-Regulation,* 6, 355-365.

Freedman, R., Ianni, P., & Wenig, P. (1983). Behavioral treatment of Raynaud's Disease. *Consulting and Clinical Psychology,* 51, 539-549.

Friar, L.R., Beatty, J. (1976). Migraine: Management by trained control of vasoconstriction. *Consulting and Clinical Psychology,* 44, 46-53.

Fried, F., Lamberti, J., & Sneed, P. (1977). Treatment of tension and migraine headaches with biofeedback techniques. *Missouri Medicine,* 74, 253-255.

Fritz, G. (1985). Cluster headaches treated with biofeedback-assisted attention training: Follow-up. *Biofeedback Society of America Proceedings,* New Orleans, Louisiana.

Furman, S. (1973). Intestinal biofeedback in functional diarrhea: A preliminary report. *Behaviour Therapy and Experimental Psychiatry,* 4, 317-321.

Furedy, J. (1979). Teaching self-regulation of cardiac function through imaginational pavlovian and biofeedback conditioning: Remember the response. In N. Birbaumer & H. Kimmel (Eds.), *Biofeedback and Self-Regulation,* 205-225. New York: John Wiley & Sons.

Furedy, J. (1985). Specific vs. placebo effects in biofeedback: Science-based vs. snake-oil behavioral medicine, *Clinical Biofeedback and Health,* 8, 155-162.

Furedy, J., & Riley, D. (1982). Classical and operant conditioning in the enhancement of biofeedback: Specifics and speculations. In L. White & B. Tursky (Eds.), *Clinical Biofeedback: Efficacy and Mechanisms,* 74-102. New York: Guilford Press.

Gamble, E., & Elder, S.T. (1983). Multimodal biofeedback in the treatment of migraine. *Biofeedback and Self-Regulation,* 8, 383-392.

Giles, S. (1981). Separate and combined effects of biofeedback training and brief individual psychotherapy in the treatment of gastrointestinal disorders. *Biofeedback Society of America Proceedings,* Louisville, Kentucky, 48.

Gladman, A. E. (1981). Awareness and self-regulation: A clinician's viewpoint. In Stephen Fahrion (Chair.), *Shifting Paradigms: Awareness, Self-Regulation, and Biofeedback,* Symposium conducted at the Biofeedback Society of America's advanced seminar, New Orleans, Louisiana.

Goldstein, I. (1982). Biofeedback in the treatment of hypertension. In L. White & B. Tursky (Ed.s), *Clinical Biofeedback: Efficacy and Mechanisms,* 142-161. New York: Guildord Press.

Goodwin, J.S., & Goodwin, J.M. (1984). The tomato effect: Rejection of highly efficacious therapies. *Journal of the American Medical Association,* 251, 2387-2390.

Green, E., & Green, A. (1977). *Beyond Biofeedback.* New York: Dell Publishing.

Green, E., Green, A., & Norris, P. (1980). Self-regulation training for control of hypertension. *Primary Cardiology,* 6, 126-137.

Green, E., Green, A., & Walters, E. D. (1970). Self-regulation of internal states. In J. Rose (Ed.), *Progress of cybernetics: Proceedings of the international congress of cybernetics,* London: Gordon & Breach.

Green, E., Sargent, J., & Walters, E. (1973). Preliminary report on the use of autogenic feedback techniques in the treatment of migraine and tension headaches. *Psychosomatic Medicine,* 35, 129-135.

Grobler, J. (1984). Biofeedback and Individual Learning Styles. *Biofeedback Society of America Proceedings,* Albuquerque, New Mexico.

Guglielmi, R.S., Roberts, A.H., & Patterson, R. (1982). Skin temperature biofeedback for Raynaud's disease: A double-blind study. *Biofeedback and Self-Regulation,* 7, 99-119.

Hafner, R.J. (1982). Psychological treatment of essential hypertension: A controlled comparison of meditation and meditation plus biofeedback. *Biofeedback and Self-Regulation,* 7, 305-315.

Hand, C., Burns, M., & Ireland, E. (1979). Treatment of hypertonicity in muscles of lip retraction. *Biofeedback and Self-Regulation,* 4, 171-181.

Hardt, J. (1975). Comment on training procedures for EEG biofeedback training. Biofeedback Research Society Meeting,

Monterey, California.

Hardyck, D., & Petrinovich, L. (1969). Treatment of subvocal speech during reading, *Journal of Reading,* 1, 1-11.

Hardyck, D., Petrinovich, L., & Ellsworth, D. (1967). Feedback of speech muscle activity during silent reading: Two comments. *Science,* 157, 579-580.

Hartje, J. & Axelberg, L. (1984). Biofeedback follow-up data for eight pathologies. *Biofeedback Society of America Proceedings,* Albuquerque, New Mexico.

Hatch, J. (1982). Controlled group designs in biofeedback research: Ask, "What does the control group control for?" *Biofeedback and Self-Regulation,* 7, 377-402.

Hatch, J., & Gatachel, (1981). The role of biofeedback in the operant modification of human heart rate. *Biofeedback and Self-Regulation,* 6, 139-167.

Hatch, J.P., Klatt, K., Fitzgerald, M., Jasheway, L.S., & Fisher, J.G. (1983). Cognitive and physiologic responses to EMG biofeedback and three types of pseudofeedback during a muscular relaxation task. *Biofeedback and Self-Regulation,* 8, 409-425.

Hauri, P. (1981). Treating psychophysiological insomnia with biofeedback. *Archives of General Psychiatry,* 38, 752-758.

Hauri, P., Percy, L., Hellekson, C., Hartmann, E., & Russ, D. (1982). The treatment of psychophysiological insomnia with biofeedback: A replication study. *Biofeedback and Self-Regulation,* 7, 223-235.

Haynes, S. (1976). Electromyographic biofeedback treatment of a woman with chronic dysphagia. *Biofeedbck and Self-Regulation,* 1, 121-124.

Haynes, S., Giffin, P., Mooney, D., & Parise, M. (1975). Electromyographic biofeedback and relaxation instructions in the treatment of muscle contraction headaches. *Behavior Therapy,* 6, 672-678.

Haynes, S.N., Mosley, D., & McGowan, W.(1975). Relaxation training and biofeedback in the reduction of frontalis muscle tension. *Psychophysiology,* 12, 547-552.

Heil, J. (1984). Imagery for sport: Theory, research, and practice. In W. Straub & J. Williams (Eds.), *Cognitive Sport Psychology,* 245-251. Lansing, New York: Sport Science

Associates.

Herzfeld, G.M.,& Taub, E., (1980). Effect of slide projections and tape-recorded suggestions on thermal biofeedback training. *Biofeedback and Self-Regulation, 5,* 393-405.

Hesse, M.B. (1970). *Models and Analogies in Science.* Notre Dame, Indiana: University of Notre Dame Press.

Hickling, E., & Sison, G. (1985). The treatment of posttraumatic stress disorder with relaxation and biofeedback training. *Biofeedback Society of America Proceedings,* New Orleans, Louisiana.

Hoelscher, T., & Lichstein, K. (1983). Blood volume pulse biofeedback treatment of chronic cluster headache. *Biofeedback and Self-Regulation, 8,* 533-540

Holroyd, K., Andrasik, F., & Noble, J. (1980). A comparison of EMG biofeedback and a credible pseudotherapy in treating tension headache. *Behavioral Medicine, 3,* 29-38.

Holroyd, K., Penzien, K., Hursey, D., Tobin, D., Rogers, Holm, J., Marcille, P., Hall, J., & Chila, A. (1984). Change mechanisms in EMG biofeedback training: Cognitive changes underlying improvements in tension headache. *Consulting and Clinical Psychology, 52,* 1039-1053.

Hoon, E.F. (1980). Biofeedback-assisted sexual arousal in females: A comparison of visual and auditory modalities. *Biofeedback and Self-Regulation, 5,* 175-191.

Horn, T. (1984). The expectancy process: Causes and consequences. In W. Straub & J. Williams (Eds.), *Cognitive Sport Psychology,* 199-211. Lansing, New York: Sports Science Associates.

Hurd, W., Pegram, V., & Nepomuceno, C. (1980). Comparison of actual and simulated EMG biofeedback in the treatment of hemiplegic patients. *American Journal of Physical Medicine, 59,* 73-82.

Hutchings, D.F., & Reinking, R.H. (1976). Tension headaches: What form of therapy is most effective? *Biofeedback and Self-Regulation, 1,* 183-190.

Hyland, M. (1985). Do person variables exist in different ways? *American Psychologist, 40,* 1003-1010.

Inz, J., & Wineburg, E. (1985). Clinical and theoretical issues of biofeedback training with the sympathectomized Raynaud's disease patient: A case study. *Biofeedback Society of America Proceedings,* New Orleans, Louisiana.

Johnson, J. & Schwartz, G. (1971). Suppression of GSR activity through operant conditioning. In J. Kamiya (Ed.), *Biofeedback and Self-Control.* Chicago: Aldine Press.

Johansson, J. & Ost, L. (1982). Self-control procedures in biofeedback: A review of temperature biofeedback in the treatment of migraine. *Biofeedback and Self-Regulation,* 7, 435-441.

Johnson, W. & Turin, A. (1975). Biofeedback treatment of migraine headache: A systematic case study. *Behavior Therapy,* 6, 294-397.

Jurish, S. Blanchard, E., Andrasik, F., Teders, S. Neff, D. & Arena, J. (1983). Home-Versus clinic-based treatment of vascular headache. *Consulting and Clinical Psychology,* 51, 741-751.

Kamiya, J. (1977). Introduction in J. Kamiya (Ed.), *Biofeedback & Self-Control,* xv-xxi, Chicago: Aldine Publishing Company.

Kappes, B., & Michaud, J. (1978). Contingent vs. noncontingent EMG feedback and hand temperature in relation to anxiety and locus of control. *Biofeedback and Self-Regulation,* 3, 51-60.

Kappes, B., & Morris, R. (1982). Thermal baseline patterns on psychiatric patients and staff. *American Journal of Clinical Biofeedback,* 5, 43-49.

Katkin, E., Fitzgerald, C., & Shapiro, D. (1978). Clinical applications of biofeedback: Current status and future prospects. In H. Pick, W. Leibowitz, J. Singer, A. Steinschneider, & H. Stevenson (Eds.), *Psychology: From research to practice.* New York: Plenum Press.

Katkin, E., & Goldband, S. (1979). The placebo effect and biofeedback. In R. Gatchel & K. Price (Ed.), *Clinical Applications of Biofeedback: Appraisal & Status,* 173-186. New York: Pergamon Press.

Keefe, F. (1982). Behavioral assessment and treatment of chronic pain: Current status and future directions. *Consulting and Clinical Psychology,* 50, 896-911.

Keefe, F.J., Surwit, R.s., & Pilon, R. (1981). Collagen vascular disease: Can behavior therapy help? *Behavior Therapy and*

Experimental Psychiatry. 12, 171-175.

Kewman, D., & Roberts, A. (1983). An alternative perspective on biofeedback efficacy studies: A reply to Steiner and Dince. *Biofeedback and Self-Regulation,* 8, 487-489.

Kewman, D., & Roberts, A. H., (1980). Skin temperature biofeedback and migraine headaches. *Biofeedback and Self-Regulation,* 5, 327-345.

Kiffer, J., Fridlun, A., & Fowler, S. (1981). Effects of alternative control procedures for electromyographic biofeedback relaxation training. *Biofeedback and Self-Regulation,* 6, 225-233.

King, A., & Arena, J. (1984). Behavioral treatment of chronic cluster headache in a geriatric patient. *Biofeedback and Self-Regulation,* 9, 201-208.

Kinsman, R.A., O'Banion, K., Robinson, S. & Staudenmayer, H. (1975). Continuous biofeedback and discrete posttrial verbal feedback in frontalis muscle relaxation training. *Psychophysiology,* 12, 30-35.

Klinge, V. (1972). Effects of exteroceptive feedback and instructions on control of spontaneous galvanic skin response. *Psychophysiology,* 9, 305-317.

Kostes, H., Rapaport, I., Glaus, K.D. (1978). Operant conditioning of skin resistance tonic levels. *Biofeedback and Self-Regulation,* 3, 43-50.

Kratochvil, D.W., Carkhuff, R. & Berenson, B. (1969). Cumulative effects of parent and teacher offered levels of facilitative conditions upon indices of student physical, emotional and intellectual functioning. *Educational Research,* 63, 161-164.

Krebs, D. (1981). Clinical electromyography feedback following meniscectomy: A multiple regression experimental analysis. *Physical Therapy,* 61, 1017-1021.

Kremsdorf, R., Kochanowicz, N., & Costell, S. (1981). Cognitive skills training versus EMG biofeedback in the reatment of tension headaches. *Biofeedback and Self-Regulation,* 6, 93-101.

Kristt, D., & Engel, B. (1975). Learned control of blood pressure in patients with high blood pressure. *Circulation,* 51, 370-378.

Lacroix, J. & Roberts, L. (1978). A comparison of the mechanisms and some properties of instructed sudomotor and cardiac control. *Biofeedback and Self-Regulation, 3,* 105-131.

Lang. P.J. (1977). Research on the specificity of feedback training: Implications for the use of biofeedback in the treatment of anxiety and fear. In J. Beatty and H. Legewie (Eds.), *Biofeedback and Behavior,* 323-330. New York: Plenum Press.

Latimer, P. (1981). Biofeedback and self-regulation in the treatment of diffuse esophageal spasm: A single-case study. *Biofeedback and Self-Regulation, 6,* 181-189.

Latimer, P., Campbell, D., & Kasperski (1984). A components analysis of biofeedback in the treatment of fecal incontinence. *Biofeedback and Self-Regulation, 9,* 311-324.

Laye, R. (1984). Skin temperature biofeedback for Raynaud's Phenomenon secondary to chain saw operation: A case study. *Biofeedback Society of America Proceedings,* Albuquerque, New Mexico.

Lazarus, R. (1975). A cognitively oriented psychologist looks at biofeedback. *American Psychologist, 30,* 553-561.

Levee, J., Cohen, J., & Rickles, W. (1976). Electromyographic biofeedback for relief of tension in the facial and throat muscles of a woodwind musician. *Biofeedback and Self-Regulation, 1,* 113-120.

LeVine, W. (1983). Behavioral and biofeedback theapy for a functionally impaired musician: A case report. *Biofeedback and Self-Regulation, 8,* 101-107.

Libo, L., & Arnold, G. (1983). Relaxation practice after biofeedback therapy: A long-term follow-up study of utilization and effectiveness. *Biofeedback and Self-Regulation, 8,* 217-227. (a)

Libo, L., & Arnold, G. (1983). Does training to criterion influence improvement? A follow-up study of EMG and thermal biofeedback. *Journal of Behavioural Medicine, 6,* 397-404.(b)

Libo, L., Arnold, G., Woodside, J., Borden, T. & Hardy, J. (1983). EMG biofeedback for functional bladder-sphincter dyssynergia: A case study. *Biofeedback and Self-Regulation, 8,* 243-253.

Love, W. , Montgomery, D. & Moeller, T. Working paper no.

1. Unpublished manuscript. Nova University: Ft. Lauderdale, Fla., 1974.

Lubar, J. & Bahler, W. (1976). Behavioral management of epileptic seizures following EEG biofeedback training of the sensorimotor rhythm. *Biofeedback and Self-Regulation,* 1, 77-104.

Lubar, J., O., & Lubar, J. F. (1984). Electroencephalographic biofeedback of SMR and Beta for treatment of attention deficit disorders in a clinical setting. *Biofeedback and Self-Regulation,* 9, 1-23.

Lutz, D., & Holmes, D., (1981). Instructions to change blood pressure and diastolic blood pressure biofeedback: Their effects on diastolic blood pressure, systolic blood pressure and anxiety. *Psychosomatic Research,* 25, 479-485.

Lynch, J., Paskewitz, D., & Orne, M. ((1974). Some factors in the feedback control of human alpha rhythm. *Psychosomatic Medicine,* 36, 399-410.

McCanne, T.R., (1983). Changes in autonomic responding to stress after practice at controlling heart rate. *Biofeedback and Self-Regulation,* 8, 9-23.

McClelland, D. (1985). *Human Motivation.* London, England: Scott Foresman & Co.

McKenzie, R. E., Ehrisman, W. J., Montgomery, P.S., & Barnes, R. H. (1974). The treatment of headache by means of electroencephalographic biofeedback. *Headache,* 13, 164-172.

Manuck, S.B., Levenson, R., Hinrichsen, J., & Gryll, S. (1975). Role of feedback in voluntary control of heart rate. *Perceptual and Motor Skills,* 40, 747-752.

Marrazo, M., Hicklin, E., & Sison, G. (1983). The psychological treatment of childhood migraine: A review and case presentation. *Biofeedback Society of America Proceedings,* Denver, Colorado.

Martinek, T. (1981). Pygmalion in the gym: A model for the communication of teacher expectations in physical education. *Research Quarterly,* 52, 58-67.

Martinek, T., & Johnson, S. (1979). Teacher expectations: Effects on dyadic interactions and self-concept in elementary age children. *Research Quarterly,* 50, 60-70.

Matheson, D., Bruce, R., & Beauchamp, K. (1974). *Introduc-*

tion to experimental psychology. New York: Holt, Rinehart & Winston.

Medina, J. L., Diamond, S., & Franklin, M. A. (1976). Biofeedback therapy for migraine. *Headache,* 16, 115-118.

Meichenbaum, D. (1976). Cognitive factors in biofeedback therapy. *Biofeedback and Self-Regulation,* 1, 201-216.

Mickelson, D. & Stevic, R. (1971). Differential effects of facilitative and non-facilitative behavioral counselors. *Counseling Psychology,* 18, 314-319.

Middaugh, S. (1978). EMG feedback as a muscle reeducation technique: A controlled study. *Physical Therapy,* 58, 15-22.

Middaugh, S., Whitehead, W., Burgio, K., & Engel, B. (1985). Biofeedback in treatment of urinary incontinence in stroke patients. *Biofeedback Society of America Proceedings,* New Orleans, Louisiana.

Miller, Neal. (1976). Clinical applications of biofeedback: Voluntary control of heart rate, rhythm, and blood pressure. In Theodore Barber (Ed.), *Biofeedback and Self-Control,* 367-377, Chicago: Aldine Publishing Company.

Miller, N. & DiCara, L. (1971). Instrumental learning of heart rate changes in curarized rats: Shaping, and specificity to discriminative stimulus. In J. Kamiya (Ed.), *Biofeedback and Self-Control,* 79-85. Chicago: Aldine Publishing.

Moeller, T. & Love, W. (1974). A method to reduce arterial hypertension through muscular relaxation. Unpublished manuscript. Nova University: Ft. Lauderdale, Fla.

Morasky, R., Reynolds, C., and Sowell, L., (1983). Generalization of lowered EMG levels during musical performance following biofeedback training. *Biofeedback and Self-Regulation,* 8, 207-217.

Moreland, V., Rosenbaum, L., & Rauseo, L. (1983). Understanding asthma: Shifts in symptoms and in systems. *Biofeedback Society of America Proceedings,* Denver, Colorado.

Nakagawa-Kogan, H., Betrus, P., Beaton, R., Burr, R., Larson, L., Mitchell, P., & Wolf-Wilets, V. (1984). Management of stress response clinic: Perspective of five years of biofeedback and self-management treatment of stress-related disorders by nurses. *Biofeedback Society of America Proceedings,* Albuquerque, New Mexico.

Neff, D. & Blanchard, E. (1985). The use of relaxation and biofeedback in the treatment of irritable bowel syndrome. *Biofeedback Society of America Proceedings,* New Orleans, Louisiana.

Nielsen, D.H., & Holmes, D.S. (1980). Effectiveness of EMG biofeedback training for controlling arousal in subsequent stressful situations. *Biofeedback and Self-Regulation,* 5, 235-245

Norton, G. (1976). Biofeedback treatment of long-standing eye closure reactions. *Behaviour Therapy and Experimental Psychiatry,* 7, 279-280.

Nouwen, A., & Solinger, J.W. (1979). The effectiveness of EMG biofeedback training in low back pain. *Biofeedback and Self-Regulation,* 4, 103-111.

O'Connell, M., & Yeaton, S.(1981). Generalized muscle changes during EMG relaxation training. *Psychophysiology,* 17, 56-61.

Olton, D.S., & Noonberg, A.R. (1980). *Biofeedback: Clinical applications in behavioral medicine.* Englewood Cliffs, New Jersey: Prentice Hall,

Onoda, L. (1983). Handwarming and relaxation in temperature biofeedback: Positive placebo effects. *Biofeedback and Self-Regulation,* 8, 109-114.

Patel, C. (1973). Yoga and bio-feedback in the management of hypertension. *Lancet,* 2, 1053-1055.

Patel, C. (1975). 12-month follow-up of yoga and bio-feedback in the management of hypertension. *Lancet,* 1, 62-64.

Patel, C. (1977). Biofeedback-aided relaxation and meditation in the management of hypertension. *Biofeedback and Self-Regulation,* 2, 1-41.

Patel, C., & Carruthers, M. (1977). Coronary risk factor reduction through biofeedback-aided relaxation and meditation. *Journal of the Royal College of General Practice,* 27, 401-405.

Patel, C., Marmot, M., & Terry, D. (1981). Controlled trial of biofeedback-aided behavioural methods in reducing mild hypertension. *British Medical Journal,* 6281, 2005-2008.

Patel, C. & North, W. (1975). Randomised controlled trial of yoga and bio-feedback in management of hypertension. *Lancet,*

2, 93-95.

Peck, D. (1977). The use of EMG feedback in the treatment of a severe case of blepharospasm. *Biofeedback and Self-Regulation,* 2, 273-277.

Perez, F., & Brown, G. (1985). The single-subject design in clinical biofeedback: A technique for the evaluation of improvement. In F. Perez (Chair), *The efficacy of single subject statistics in evaluating clinical biofeedback.* Symposium presented at the Biofeedback Society of America Annual Meeting, New Orleans, Louisiana.

Philips, C. (1977). The modification of tension headache pain using EMG biofeedback. *Behaviour Research and Therapy,* 15, 119-129.

Plotkin, W. (1977). On the social psychology of experiential states associated with EEG alpha biofeedback training. In J. Beatty and H. Legewie (Eds.) *Biofeedback and Behavior,* 121-134. New York: Plenum Press.

Plotkin, W., & Cohen, R. (1976). Occipital alpha and the attributes of the "alpha experience," *Psychophysiology,* 13, 16-21.

Plotkin, W., Mazer, C., & Loewy (1976). Alpha enhancement and the likelihood of an alpha experience, *Psychophysiology,* 13, 466-471.

Price, K. (1979). Biofeedbck and migraine, In R. Gatchel & K. Price (Ed.), *Clinical Applications of Biofeedback: Appraisal & Status,* 28-51. New York: Pergamon Press.

Price. K., & Tursky, B. (1976). Vascular reactivity of migraineurs and non-migraineurs: A comparison of responses to self-control procedures. *Headache,* 16, 210-217.

Raskin, M., Johnson, G. & Rondestvedt, J. (1973). Chronic anxiety treated by feedback-induced muscle relaxation: A pilot study. *Archives of General Psychiatry,* 28, 263-266.

Reeves, J. (1976). EMG-Biofeedback reduction of tension headache: A cognitive skills training approach. *Biofeedback and Self-Regulation,* 1, 217-225.

Reinking, R. & Kohl, M., (1975). Effects of various forms of relaxation training on physiological and self-report measures of relaxation. *Consulting and Clinical Psychology,* 43, 595-600.

Roberts, A. (1985). Biofeedback. *American Psychologist,* 40,

938-941.

Roberts, A., Kewman, D., & MacDonald, H. (1973). Voluntary control of skin temperature: Unilateral changes using hypnosis and feedback. *Abnormal Psychology,* 1, 163-168.

Rosenbaum, L. (1983). Biofeedbck-assisted stress management for insulin-treated diabetes mellitus. *Biofeedback and Self-Regulation,* 8, 519-532.

Rosenbaum, L., Greco, P., Sternberg, C., & Singleton, G. (1981). Ongoing assessment: Experience of a university biofeedback clinic. *Biofeedback and Self-Regulation,* 6, 103-111.

Runck, B. (1980). *Biofeedback—Issues in treatment assessment* (Department of Health and Human Services No. 80-1032). Rockville, MD: National Institute of Mental Health.

Ryle, G. (1949). *The Concept of Mind.* New York: Barnes and Noble.

Ryle, G. (1965). Categories. In A. Flew, (Ed.) *Logic and Language.* Garden City, New York: Doubleday, 281-299.

Sargent, J., Walters, E, & Green, E. (1973). Psychosomatic self-regulation of migraine headaches. *Seminars in Psychiatry,* 5, 415-428.

Schneider, C., Osterberg, G., McConnell, J., & Stevenson, M.L. (1983). Description and comparison of clinical methods and results in the treatment of four psychosomatic disorders. Symposium presented at the Biofeedback Society of America meeting,

Schwartz, G. (1972). Voluntary control of human cardiovascular integration and differentiation through feedback and reward. *Science,* 175, 90-93.

Schwartz, G. & Shapiro, D. (1973). Biofeedback and essential hypertension: Current findings and theoretical concerns. In L. Birk (Ed.), *Biofeedback: Behavioral Medicine.* New York: Grune & Strattton.

Schwartz, G. Shapiro, D., & Tursky, B. (1971). Learned control of cardiovascular integration in man through operant conditioning, In J. Kamiya (Ed.), *Biofeedback and Self-Control,* 245-250. Chicago: Aldine Press.

Sedlacek, K. (1979). Biofeedback for Raynaud's disease. *Psychosomatics,* 10, 535-541.

Sedlacek, K., & Cohen, J. (1978). Biofeedback and the treatment of essential hypertension. *Proceedings of the Biofeedback Society of America Ninth Annual Meeting,* 274-276.

Sedlacek, K., Cohen, J., & Boxhill, C. (1979). Comparison between biofeedback and relaxation response in the treatment of essential hypertension. Biofeedback Society of America Proceedings, 84-87. San Diego, California.

Segreto-Bures, J., & Kotses, H. (1984). Effects of noncontingent feedback on EMG training, EMG responses, and subjective experience. *Biofeedback and Self-Regulation,* 9, 25-35.

Sellick, S. & Fitzsimmons, G. (1983). Long-Term effects of having demonstrated a specific preset level of skill acquisition during biofeedback training for the relief of migraine headaches. *Biofeedback Society of America Proceedings,* 200-201, Denver, Colorado.

Shannon, B., Goldman, M., & Lee, R. (1978). Biofeedback training of blood pressure: A comparison of three feedback techniques, *Psychophysiology,* 15, 53-59.

Shapiro, D., & Goldstein, I. (1982). Biobehavioral perspectives on hypertension. *Consulting and Clinical Psychology,* 50, 841-858.

Shapiro, D., & Surwit, R. (1976). Learned control of physiological function and disease. In H. Leitenberg (Ed.), *Handbook of behavior modification and behavior therapy.* Englewood Cliffs, New Jersey: Prentice-Hall.

Shapiro, D., Tursky, B., Gershon, E., & Stern, M. (1971). Effects of feedback and reinforcement on the control of human systolic blood pressure. In J. Kamiya (Ed.), *Biofeedback and Self-Control.* Chicago: Aldine Press.

Shapiro, D., & Watanabe, T., (1972). Timing characteristics of operant electrodermal modification: Fixed-interval effects. In D. Shapiro (Ed.), *Biofeedback and Self-Control,* 311-318. Chicago: Aldine Publishing.

Sharpley, C. & Rogers, J. (1984). A meta-analysis of frontalis EMG levels with biofeedback and alternative procedures. *Biofeedback and Self-Regulation,* 9, 385-394.

Shaw, E. R., & Blanchard, E. G. (1983). The effects of instructional set on the outcome of a stress management program. *Biofeedback and Self-Regulation,* 8, 555-566.

Shellenberger, R. (1984). The ghost in the box. In R. Shellenberger

(Chair.), *When does biofeedback training succeed and when does it fail?* Panel conducted at the Biofeedback Society of America Meeting, Albuquerque, New Mexico.

Shellenberger, R. (1984). Reliabilty and validity issues in stress profiling. In Harold Musiker (Chair.), *Profiling and Assessment, Evaluation and Treatment of Various Physiopathological Conditions.* Symposium conducted at the Biofeedback Society of America meeting, Albuquerque, New Mexico.

Shellenberger, R. & Lewis, M. (1986). Reliability of stress profiling, in *Biofeedback Society of America Proceedings*, San Francisco, California.

Shellenberger, R., Turner, J., Green, J., & Cooney, J. (1986). Health changes in a biofeedback and stress management program, *Clinical Biofeedack and Health*, 9, 23-34.

Shellenberger, R., Green, J., Cooney, J., & Turner, J. (1983). *Stress profiling: A procedure for assessing the effectiveness of stress management programs and predicting disease patterns.* Denver, Colorado: Colorado Commission on Higher Education.

Shirley, M., Burish, G. & Rowe, C. (1982). Effectiveness of multiple-site EMG biofeedback in the reduction of arousal. *Biofeedback and Self-Regulation*, 7, 167-184.

Shulimson, A., Lawrence, P., Iacono, C. (1985). Diabetic ulcers: The effect of thermal biofeedback training on healing. *Biofeedback Society of America Proceedings*, New Orleans, Louisiana.

Simpson, D.D., & Nelson, A. E., (1976). Specificity of finger pulse volume feedback during relaxation. *Biofeedback and Self-Regulation*, 1, 433-443.

Smoll, F., & Smith, R. (1984). Leadership research in youth sports. In J. Silva III & R. Weinberg (Eds.), *Psychological Foundations of Sport.*, 371-385. Champaign, Ill: Human Kinetics Publishing.

Solbach, P., & Sargent, J. (1977). A follow-up evaluation of the Menninger pilot migraine study using thermal training. *Headache*, 17, 198-202.

Stanwood, J., Lanyon, R., & Wright, M. (1984). Treatment of severe hemifacial spasm with biofeedback: A case study.

Behavior Modification, 8, 567-580.

Steiner, S., & Dince., W. (1981). Biofeedback efficacy studies: A critique of critiques. *Biofeedback and Self-Regulation*, 6, 275-288.

Steiner, S. & Dince, W., (1983). A reply on the nature of biofeedback efficacy studies. *Biofeedback and Self-Regulation*, 8, 499-504.

Stephens, J., Harris, A., & Brady, J. (1972). Large magnitude heart rate changes in subjects instructed to change their heart rates and given exteroceptive feedback. *Psychophysiology*, 9, 283-285.

Sterman, M. B. (1985). SMR update: Six long-term cases of EEG biofeedback treatment in epilepsy. Presentation at Biofeedback Society of America Conference, New Orleans, Louisiana.

Sterman, M. B. (1973). Neurophysiologic and clinical studies of sensorimotor EEG biofeedback training: Some effects on epilepsy. In L. Birk (Ed.), *Biofeedback: Behavioral Medicine*, 147-165. New York: Grune & Stratton.

Sterman, M.B. (1978). Sensorimotor EEG operant conditioning: Experimental and clinical effects. *Pavlovian Journal of Biological Science*, 12, 63-92.

Sterman, M.B., & MacDonald, L. (1978) Effects of central cortical EEG feedback training on incidence of poorly controlled seizures. *Epilepsia*, 19, 207-222.

Sterman, M.B., MacDonald, L., & Stone, R. (1974). Biofeedback training of the sensorimotor EEG rhythm in man: Effects on epilepsy. *Epilepsia*, 15, 395-416.

Stern, G.S., & Berrenberg, J.L. (1977). Biofeedback training in frontalis muscle relaxation and enhancement of belief in personal control. *Biofeedback and Self-Regulation*, 2, 173-182.

Stoffer, G., Jensen, J., & Nesset, B. (1979). Effects of contingent versus yoked temperature feedback on voluntary temperature control and cold stress tolerance. *Biofeedback and Self-Regulation*, 4, 541-562.

Stoyva, J. & Budzynski, T. (1974). Cultivated low arousal—an antistress response? In L. DiCara (Ed.), *Biofeedback and Self-Control*, 265-290. Chicago: Aldine Publishing.

Stroebel, C. & Glueck. D. (1973). Biofeedback—The Ultimate

Placebo? In L. Birk (Ed.), *Biofeedback: Behavioral Medicine*, New York: Grune & Stratton.

Sturgis, E., Tollison, D., & Adams, H. (1978). Modification of combined migraine-muscle contraction headaches using BVP and EMG feedback. *Applied Behavior Analysis*, 11, 215-223.

Suinn, R. (1984). Imagery and Sports. In W. Straub & J. Williams (Eds.), *Cognitive Sports Psychology*, 253-270. Lansing, New York: Sport Science Associates.

Surwit, R. (1982). Round-Table discussion of Beatty, Surwit, and Blanchard in L. White and B. Tursky (Eds.), Clinical Biofeedback: Efficacy and Mechanisms. New York: Guilford Press.

Surwit, R., & Shapiro, D. (1976). Biofeedback and meditation in the treatment of borderline hypertension. Paper presented at the annual meeting of the American Psychosomatic Society, Pittsburg.

Surwit, R., Shapiro, D., & Good, M. (1978). Comparison of cardiovascular biofeedback, neuromuscular biofeedback, and meditation in the treatment of borderline essential hypertension. *Consulting and Clinical Psychology*, 45, 252-263.

Suter, S., Fredericson, M., & Portuesi, L. (1983). Mediation of skin temperature biofeedback effects in children. *Biofeedback and Self-Regulation*, 8, 567-584.

Tansey, M., & Bruner, R. (1983). EMG and EEG biofeedback training in the treatment of a 10-year-old hyperactive boy with a developmental reading disorder. *Biofeedback and Self-Regulation*, 8, 25-37.

Taub, E. (1977). Self-regulation of human tissue temperature. In G. E. Schwartz & J. Beatty (Eds.), *Biofeedback Theory and Research*, 265-300. Nw York: Academic Press Inc.

Thompson, J. K., Raczynski, J., Habaer, J., & Strugis, E. (1983). The control issue in biofeedback training. *Biofeedback and Self-Regulation*, 8, 153-164.

Toscano, W., & Cowings, P. (1982). Reducing motion sickness: A comparison of autogenic-feedback training and an alternative cognitive task. *Aviation, Space and Environmental Medicine*, May, 449-453.

Truax, C. B., & Mitchell, K.M. (1971). Research on certain therapist interpersonal skills in relation to process and outcome, In A. Bergin & S. Garfield (Eds.), *Handbook of Psychotherapy and Behavior Change.* New York: Wiley.

Turin, A., and Johnson, W. (1976). Biofeedback therapy for migraine headaches. *Archives of General Psychiatry,* 33, 517-519.

Twentyman, C. & Lang, P. (1980). Instructed heart rate control: Effects of varying feedback frequency and timing. *Biofeedback and Self-Regulation,* 4, 417-425.

Uchiyama, K., Lutterjohann, M., & Shah, D. (1981). Crosscultural differences in frontalis muscle tension levels: An exploratory study comparing Japanese and Westerners. *Biofeedback and Self-Regulation,* 6, 75-78. Volow, M., Erwin, C., Cipolat, A. (1979). Biofeedback control of skin potential level. *Biofeedback and Self-Regulation,* 4, 133-143.

Volow, C., Erwin, C., Cipolat, A. (1979). Biofeedback control of skin potential level. *Biofeedback and Self-Regulation,* 4, 133-143.

Wald, A. (1981). Use of biofeedback in the treatment of fecal incontinence in patients with menineomyelocele. *Pediatrics,* 68, 45-49.

Weinman, M., Scenchuk, K.M., Gaebe, G. & Matthew, R.J. (1983). The effect of stressful life events on EMG biofeedback and relaxation training in the treatment of anxiety. *Biofeedback and Self-Regulation,* 8, 191-205.

Wells, D. (1973) Large magnitude voluntary heart rate changes. *Psychophysiology,* 3, 260-269.

Weinberg, R. (1984). Mental preparation strategies, In J. Silva III & R. Weinberg (Eds.), *Psychological Foundations of Sport.* 145-156. Champaign, Ill: Human Kinetics Publishing.

Wickramasekera, I. (1978). Instructions and EMG feedback in systematic desensitization: A case report. *Biofeedback, Behavior Therapy, and Hypnosis.* 91-98. Chicago: Nelson-Hall.

Wiedel, T. (1985). Biofeedback and relaxation training for post-traumatic stress disorder: Two years of treatment activities recounted. *Biofeedback Society of America Proceedings,* New Orleans, Louisiana.

Whitsett, S., Lubar, J., Holder, G., Pamplin, W., & Shabsin, H. (1982). A double-blind investigation of the relationship between seizure activity and the sleep EEG following EEG biofeedback training. *Biofeedback and Self-Regulation,* 7, 193-210.

Willerman, L., Skeen, J. & Simpson, J. (1978). Retention of learned temperature changes during problem solving. In J. Stoyva (Ed.), *Biofeedback and Self-Control,* 504-510. New York: Aldine Publishing.

Williamson, D.A., Janell, M.P., Marguelot, J.E., & Hutchinson, P. (1983). Comparisons of high, medium, and low feedback sensitivity for the control of heart acceleration. *Biofeedback and Self-Regulation,* 8, 39-44.

Wilson, V.E., & Bird, E.I. (1981). Effects of relaxation and/or biofeedback training upon hip flexion in gymnasts. *Biofeedback and Self-Regulation,* 6, 25-34.

Wolf, S., Baker, M., & Kelly, J. (1980). EMG biofeedback in stroke: A one year follow-up on the effect of patient characteristics. *Archives of Physical Medicine and Rehabilitation,* 61, 351-355.

Wolf, S., Nacht, M., & Kelly, J. (1982). EMG feedback training during dynamic movement for low back pain patients. *Behaviour Therapy,* 13, 395-406.

Yates, A. J. (1980). Biofeedback and the modification of behavior. New York: Plenum Press.

Yock, T. (1983). Follow-up study of a university based biofeedback treatment program. In Carol Schneider (Chair.), *Biofeedback in Educational Settings.* Symposium conducted at the Biofeedback Society of America meeting, Denver, Colorado.